30 Days in Sydney

The Fat Man in History
Bliss
Illywhacker
Oscar and Lucinda
The Tax Inspector
The Unusual Life of Tristan Smith
The Big Bazhooley
Jack Maggs
True History of the Kelly Gang

30 Days in Sydney

A wildly distorted account

Peter Carey

BLOOMSBURY

First published 2001

Copyright © 2001 by Peter Carey

The moral right of the author has been asserted

Bloomsbury Publishing Plc,
38 Soho Square, London WID 3HB

A CIP catalogue record for this book
is available from the British Library

ISBN 0 7475 5500 1

10 9 8 7 6 5 4

Typeset by Hewer Text Ltd, Edinburgh
Printed by Clays Ltd, St Ives plc

For Kelvin, Lester, Sheridan,
Marty, Jack and Geordie

'I had to rearrange their faces
and give them all another name.'

CHAPTER ONE

I DESPAIR OF BEING able to convey to any reader
my own idea of the beauty of Sydney Harbour,
wrote Anthony Trollope. I have seen nothing
equal to it in the way of landlocked scenery, –
nothing, second to it. Dublin Bay, the Bay of
Spezia, New York and the Cove of Cork are all
picturesquely fine. Bantry Bay, with the nooks of
the sea running up to Glengarrif, is very lovely.
But they are not the equal of Sydney either in
shape, in colour, or in variety. I have never seen
Naples, or Rio Janeiro, or Lisbon; – but from the
description and pictures I am led to think that
none of them can possess such a world of loveliness of water as lies within Sydney Heads.

I could not see the harbour from the aisle seat
of the Boeing 747 that brought me home from
New York and I squirmed and craned just like

my broad-shouldered companions from Connecticut, each dressed in spectacular outfits tailored
from the stars and stripes. Members of a martial-
arts team, they were so aflame about this journey,
had been *loudly* excited since we left LA thirteen
hours before, that they had tested the powers of
my Temazepam to the limits. It had taken two
15mg capsules and four glasses of red wine
before I could finally sleep. Our conversations
had been brief. I knew only that they wished to
win some medals in Sydney. They knew that I
lived in New York City. I am sure they had no
idea that I was an Australian trying to get a
glimpse of home.

Home? I did not come to live in Sydney until I
was almost forty and even then I carried in my
baggage a typical Melbournian distrust of that
vulgar crooked convict town. I rented a leaking
ramshackle semi in Balmain because I knew that
even if my mother was correct, even if Sydney
was just like Liberace, I could never be sorry to
wake in the morning and look out on that harbour. This was in Wharf Road, Balmain, between
Stannard's shipyard and the Caltex terminal.
Balmain was an old working-class suburb with
vanilla slices in the bakers' windows, bad restaurants, bleak beer-sour pubs patronised by dock
workers, communists, crims, cops and the odd

mythologiser who wistfully described its literary life to a reporter from *Le Monde* as 'Le Ghetto de Balmain'.

There were writers, yes, but in those years Balmain had a working waterfront and at the bottom of my neglected garden I could watch the low-riding brown work boats, oil tankers, container ships, and smell the fuel oil and watch the flying foxes swooping like Tolkien's Nazguls in the hot subtropical nights when Margot Hutcheson, who I lived with in those years, slept beside me on a mattress right on the harbour's edge. The oily iridescent dark throbbed with the sounds of ships' generators.

Now, twenty-seven years later, a resident alien in the United States, I was making claim on the city 2,000 feet below. The video display showed Sydney only three miles distant, but the choppy Pacific was still obscured by low cloud and when we finally broke through, I didn't know where I was. We could not take the perfect flight path I had dreamed of, one which would bring me straight into the familiar mouth of Sydney, between those two high yellow bluffs they call the Heads.

These bright yellow cliffs show the city's DNA – that is, it is a sandstone city, and sandstone shows everywhere amongst the black and khaki bush, in the convict buildings of old Sydney and

3

in the retaining walls of all those steep harbour-side streets. Sydney sandstone has many qualities. It is soft and easily worked (to the convicts a sandstone was a man who cried and broke beneath the lash). It is also highly porous, and the first settlers would use it to filter water. When it rains in Sydney, which it does as dramatically as a Hong Kong monsoon, the water drains rapidly, leaving a thin dry topsoil from which the nutrients have long ago been leached. This in turn determines the unique flora which thrives here.

With nutrients so scarce, Tim Flannery writes, plants can't afford to lose leaves to herbivores. As a result they defend their foliage with a deadly cocktail of toxins and it's these toxins that give the bush its distinctive smell – the antiseptic aroma of the eucalypts and the pungent scent of the mint bush. When the leaves of such plants fall to the ground the decomposers in the soil often find it difficult to digest them, for they are laden with poisons. The dead leaves thus lie on the rapidly draining sand until a very hot spell. Then, fanned by searing north winds, there is fire.

So the very perfume of the Sydney air is a consequence of sandstone. It is also sandstone that dictates the terms of human settlement. For 40,000 years Aboriginal hunters and gatherers had known how to eat, to sometimes feast here, but the British who began their creeping invasion in 1788 had no clue of where they were. They set out to farm as they might in Kent or Surrey and the sandstone nearly killed them for it. Starvation. That is what the yellow cliffs of Sydney spell if you wish to read them. But there is more, much more. This modern good-time city of beaches and restaurants, of sailing boats and boozy Friday nights, was formed by traumas that it cloaks so casually you might easily miss them. If you come from New York City all you may notice is the apparent easiness of life, the lightness, the sense of a population forever on holiday. But there was a bitter war fought here upon and about this earth. The Eora tribe, who still thought of Sydney as their country, were given smallpox and fell like flies. Convicts were flogged. Convicts raped Eora women. Eora men trapped and murdered convicts. Two hundred years later the past continues to insist itself upon the present in ways that are dazzlingly and almost unbelievably clear.

Of course Captain Cook never recommended that anyone settle in Sydney Cove. It was Botany Bay, five miles to the south, that he promoted as a place of settlement, but Governor Phillip took one look at Botany Bay and declared it impossible. Within a week he had inspected Sydney Harbour and set his human cargo ashore.

His Excellency, wrote Watkin Tench, seeing the state these poor objects [the convicts] were in, ordered a piece of ground to be enclosed, for the purposes of raising vegetables for them. The seeds that were sown upon this occasion, on first appearing above ground, looked promising and well, but soon withered away.

It is more than a little intriguing that some of the best vegetable gardens in Sydney can be found today at Botany Bay, and one is tempted to imagine how the city might have formed, how its character would be different, if Governor Phillip had settled where he had been instructed.

But Botany Bay was abandoned, and, one feels in looking at it, *punished* for not being what Cook had promised. It became the place where everything and everyone who is not wanted – the dead, mad, criminal, and merely indigenous – could be tucked away, safely out of sight. It is the back yard, the back door, the place where human shit is dumped. What better place to site an airport?

On the day I arrived in search of home I skimmed low across the choppy waters of Botany Bay, and landed with a hard unpleasant bump at Kingsford Smith Sydney International Airport.

Customer O'Brien, Customer Figgis. These were the first words I heard spoken on Australian soil.

Customer O'Brien, Customer Figgis, please present yourselves at the podium inside the terminal.

The formal bureaucratic style jarred my ears and reminded me that I was indeed home, no wucking furries!

Customer O'Brien, approach the podium.

I turned to my companions from Connecticut. They did not know how weird they looked. Nor did they have the least idea of what a strange place they were in. Of course they were not offended by this style of greeting but I was suddenly awash with irritation more explicable in a teenager coming home from boarding school and discovering the unsuitability of his family. God damn! Why did we talk to people like this? *Customer?* What sort of dreary meeting in what windowless conference room had produced this honorific for international travellers? *Customer O'Brien. Customer Kane!*

You cannot expect a curious tourist to understand that this language contains the secrets of our history, but this was the discourse of a nation which began its life without a bourgeoisie, whose first citizens learned the polite mode of conversation from police reports: eg, At this stage I apprehended the suspect, I informed him of his rights and he come quietly with me to the podium where he assisted me with my enquiries.

Yes, this is unfair of me. The word *customer* is decent enough. You are our *customer*. If you are a *customer*, then you shall be served. But, damn it, we have always had trouble with service.

In 1958 the Englishman J.D. Pringle, in his patronising but insightful *Australian Accent*, made the following useful observation of Australians: they are inclined to assume that being polite is to be servile.

One could give many examples of this, he continues. Lawrence described it perfectly in the opening pages of *Kangaroo* when Somers is trying to get a taxi. A distinguished British scientist who was staying in a small hotel during a visit to Australia once asked the hotel porter – or man of all work – to bring down his bags from his room. He was taken aback to be told: 'Why don't yer do it yerself – yer look big enough.' . . . The Australian cannot see why a man should not carry his own bags if he is strong enough to do so. The same reasoning lies behind the almost universal custom of sitting in the front of the taxi if you are alone. To sit behind would imply the master-servant relationship of the rich man and his chauffeur. The driver will not say anything if you sit in the back, but he will often manage to make you feel that you have committed an error of taste.

Pringle seems unable to actually say *why* the porter and the taxi driver might be like this. At first I was irritated by this apparent obtuseness but finally, in the last page of his book, I began to suspect that his silence was produced by caution. He had worked in Sydney after all. He knew better than to say that its inhabitants were still marked by *the convict stain*. But, in the last lines of *Australian Accent*, he finally reveals what has been on his mind for 202 pages. Deep in the secret heart of Sydney, he writes, beneath the brashness and the pride and the boasting, is a memory of human suffering, and a resentment of those who caused it.

The past in Sydney is like this, both celebrated and denied, buried yet everywhere in evidence as in this Exhibit A, this irritating honorific *Customer*, which I set before Your Honour as, on this clear blue-skied morning, I come to claim a home.

CHAPTER TWO

IF YOU CAN CONFIDENTLY say you know a city, you are probably talking about a town. A metropolis is, by definition, inexhaustible, and by the time I departed, thirty days later, Sydney was as unknowable to me as it had been on that clear April morning when I arrived. As the final heat of summer waned and we moved into the cool sunny days of May, I would make more than my fair share of discoveries, and yet I would leave with pretty much the same notions I arrived with – Sydney was like no other place on earth, and it was defined not only by its painful and peculiar human history but also by the elements: Earth, Air, Fire and Water.

You can live in New York all your life and, give or take a blizzard or two, somehow persuade yourself that nature does not apply to you. I

would never seek to define Manhattan by asking
my New York friends for stories of Earth and Air
and Fire and Water, but that is exactly what was
in my mind as I walked through Immigration at
Kingsford Smith Sydney International Airport. It
was a nice simple idea and I could head for EXIT
B totally confident of the wealth of material that
awaited me.

I was expecting Kelvin, and he was there, a
heavy-set fellow in a crumpled beige suit. He was
there because he was my oldest dearest friend but
he also happens to be a perfect example of what I
mean. He knows things about Water that I am
happy to be hearing on dry land.

Kelvin waves his rolled *Financial Review*
above the crowd and as he pushes towards me
I must confess that I have changed his name, not
for any legal reason, but because I have employed
him as a character before and if you watch that
slight rise of colour above the size seventeen neck,
if you observe those shoulders forcing their way
through the press, you will easily guess that this is
a man who would not quietly accept imprison-
ment on the page. Kelvin actually enjoys being
written about, but he is very particular about his
portraits. He meddles. He drinks with editors.
Such are his connections that he has been able,
without my knowledge or consent, to eradicate

whole paragraphs between proof and first edition.

Kelvinator? he says when I tell him his name. What sort of fucking name is that?

Built like a refrigerator, I explain. It's very flattering.

He has aged since he first arrived at my door in 1974. He no longer has the shoulder-length blond hair or the shark's tooth round his naked neck but, on hearing his *nom de guerre*, he reveals that his mouth, mobile, sentimental, quarrelsome, is quite unchanged.

I am going to call him Kelvinator even if he hates it, but in return I will give him a little extra hair. He should be grateful. He is a middle-aged man in a crumpled suit, and it is in my power to make him bald.

Kelvinator? he says. We'll discuss this later.

So saying he snatches up my bag and starts for the car park.

Wait, I need to change some money.

Forget it. You've got a problem here you don't want to have.

I don't have a problem.

Yes you do. Sheridan is here. He's stalking you.

How could I guess that it was Sheridan who would finally blow my simple ideas wide apart and demand my story should be about him?

I like Sheridan, I said innocently, as I searched the crowd for a sign of that untidy bearded face.

No, mate, said Kelvin, taking me firmly by the elbow and propelling me past Foreign Exchange and out into that bright clear Sydney air. No, mate, the old Sherry is very drunk. He is in no state for pleasant conversation.

It's seven o'clock.

Exactly. I told him you arrived yesterday and I thought you were staying at the Regent but he's still lurching around the arrivals hall.

We can't just leave him here.

Mate, said Kelvin, relax. His older son is with him and he, thank Christ, is almost sober. You really wouldn't want to deal with this straight off the plane. Sheridan's broken up with Clara and he's been living in a cave in the mountains.

Oh I'm sorry.

Well it's probably very nice for Clara. He's got himself obsessed with Aboriginal firestick farming. It's all he can talk about. He had a great pile of notes to give you. He drops them. The son picks them up. There's not a lot of variety in the act.

Well I'd like to read about firestick farming.

According to Sheridan the whole issue is a conspiracy by the mining companies.

To what end?

Who would have any fucking idea? I can't see my car.

I followed him as he searched through row after row of shining new and near-new vehicles. Perhaps it was just that JFK is so ugly and chaotic, or perhaps it was the smell of eucalyptus in the air, but even here in an airport car park Sydney seemed particularly unpressured and attractive. It was seven in the morning. Everything seemed clean and uncongested. There was a gentle nor'-easterly blowing. There were flowering shrubs and, again, that clear crystal warble of the western magpies.

Halfway down a row of cars headlights flashed and a horn hooted. Ha, cried Kelvin, there she blows.

Jesus, Kelvin, that's a Jaguar.

It's just a little one, he giggled.

It was not a little one and it was ridiculous that Kelvin should own any size of Jaguar at all. When I first knew him he had spent three years on the dole, just catching waves at Nambucca Heads. He had worked for Mother Teresa in India. He had drawn a comic strip called 'The Bong Brothers' which was much loved by all my friends, but when he lived in my house he could not even pay the rent. Yet somehow, twenty-five years later, he was the publisher of fifteen suburban newspapers and five special-interest magazines. He was the CEO of a publicly listed company. He was also a member of a syndicate heavily invested in an IPO (an Initial Public Offering of shares). He was worth 24 mill or 30 mill which was, of course, impossible.

I first met Kelvin after I moved from one side of Snails Bay to the other, to what the taxi drivers called Lousy Road because it was so narrow. Louisa Road was low-rent waterfront on Sydney Harbour with no real downside except the brutal westerly winds and the weeks when the rusting hulks which were sometimes moored across the bottom of our yards left their generators running through the night.

On the corner of the entrance to the street there was a brothel with plentiful parking beneath. At the other end, just by the ferry wharf, was the house one of my neighbours rented to an outlaw motor-cycle gang, and in the middle was a shipyard, a boat builder, a mixture of tradespeople who worked at the naval dockyard on Cockatoo Island, a taxi driver, an art conservator, a plumber, a writer or two, a heroin addict with no regular occupation, some general bohemians, and people like myself and Kelvin who saw my red Jensen Healey and made enquiries.

It would take years for Kelvin to begin to accept that I might be a writer.

You're in advertising? he asked me that first night. Apart from the large manila envelope under his arm he looked like the surfie he had sometimes been. I'm wondering, mate, he said, if you could spare a moment of your time.

The manila envelope contained the dummy of a weekly newspaper; the one thing he needed was, well, some advertising.

They were different times. He did not begin by predicting circulation. This, he said, as he pulled the dummy copy from the envelope, is going to blow the power structure wide open.

In April of the year 2000 I slid into the leather-rich world of his Jaguar. How's the stock market? I asked.

He grinned. Down three per cent.

You could sell, I suggested. You'd still be well ahead.

Nah, can't do that, mate. Too many people depending on me. Who? Well silly bloody Sheridan for one.

He bought into the IPO? You told *me* not to.

I told *him* not to. But he thought I was being cagey, and he bought a lot.

How many?

Every zac he had. Eight thou.

What are they worth now?

Do me a favour – don't even talk about this.

We drove in silence from the airport. I thought of Sheridan, who was a large ebullient man, so filled with energy and affection. It was terrible to think of him really unhinged, and I quietly resolved to get in contact with him that day.

Just enjoy being back, said Kelvin. You're on a jet-lag high. This is the moment when everything looks perfect.

The freeway has changed.

It's the Olympics. Everything's changed.

But look at all these flowering trees. They're just so beautiful. You know, I'd forgotten, but we do have the most astonishing plants.

Jet-lag high.

They're strange and prehistoric. That's a hakea, right? I'd forgotten I knew its name. That's a callistemon, that's a grevillea. It's just great to know the names of things again. I've been reading this book by Flannery. I'll lend it to you.

Got no time to read, mate.

OK, this is a fire landscape. These are the fire-loving plants. Fire is one of the things that make this town so different.

Yes, tell me about it. I still miss that house at Taylors Bay. I never want to see a fire like that again.

Maybe you could tell me about that fire, for the book.

What? And be called Kelvinator? No thanks, mate. He pointed to the red bottle-brush flowers as we whizzed past. That's a callistemon if you're interested.

Yes, and that's a *Grevillea robusta*.

Leptospermum.

It's odd we use the Latin names, I said, as he planted his foot and the V12 engine took us between the khaki scrub, the spidery flowers. We were flying at 120 kilometres an hour. We have so much flora, I said, so many species, but hardly any common names. We are an anti-intellectual people who speak in Latin. I wonder what they were really called.

Kelvin was threading in and out of traffic and he did not look at me but I could feel him bristling. What do you mean, 'really'?

Previously, I said, before 1788.

The country was more real before 1788?

Don't get so quarrelsome so fast. I meant, what did the Eora people name these plants?

We were approaching the first traffic lights where the intense botanical show faded away and Moore Park Road stretched before us. Now, as he slowed, Kelvin looked across at me and rolled his eyes.

Listen, he said, I am all for Aboriginal land rights.

Good.

And I wish this little turd of a prime minister could be big enough to apologise to the Aboriginals for all the dreadful shit they've suffered, but this is my country too. I know what I call grevillea. And I don't give a fuck what it was called before. I have no fucking interest, Pete. This is a big city. We've got four million people. We've got so much other more important shit to deal with.

Well I guess the Eora don't give a fuck either.

There was a war, that's what I told Sheridan. There was a war, mate. Our side won. All through history there have been wars for territory. I think that's been our big mistake, to never admit that there was a war, to pretend that we found this nice empty bit of land that no one happened to be using. We were raised on lies and it's a shock for people to recognise the truth. I don't mean the Aboriginals, they've known all along.

After that we drove in silence, as we came down on to Moore Park Road beside which a great swathe of green stretched luxuriously to the horizon.

What do you think this road was 'really' called? he grinned.

Shut up, Kelvin.

No, there was a road here, Pete, or at least it was a path at first.

How would you know a thing like that?

As a matter of fact, I learned it this morning, waiting for your plane.

Sheridan?

He says that tens of thousands of years ago, there was a cliff beneath Moore Park Road or Anzac Parade, he wasn't sure which one. Anyway the Kooris had a path along the edge of the cliff from Sydney Cove to Botany Bay. Then the sands blew in from the east and the land was flat but people are creatures of habit so the footpath continued to follow the line of the cliff. For tens of thousands of years this track was used and by the time Sheridan's great-great-grandfather was nabbed for forging contracts it had become a cart track. And now it is Moore Park Road.

You think that's true?

Sheridan is a fucking disaster, but yes, probably.

Soon we had turned off Moore Park Road and I guess it was the jet-lag high for, as I passed through Centennial Park and into Woollahra, beneath huge Moreton Bay figs, along street after street of Victorian cast iron, I thought that I had never been in such a beautiful city in my life.

Did you choose this route on purpose?

But Kelvin did not even understand my question. He was in a hurry now. He had a meeting with his fellow syndicate members who were nervous about this falling market.

What are you going to do today? he asked, as he pulled into the lane and yanked my case out of the boot.

CHAPTER THREE

HERE IS THE KEY to the house, said Kelvinator, and here is the key to the old Honda which is parked in the street. Use it as if it was your own. Here is the burglar-alarm code, don't lose it, and will you be eating with us tonight, no, don't worry, call me at work when you make up your mind. Janet will be back from Melbourne around lunchtime. The kids will be home at four but they can let themselves in.

He left to face his board. And I stood in the middle of his newly renovated kitchen worrying about Sheridan. Like most of my Sydney friends Sheridan drank too much red wine, was argumentative and opinionated. Yet he was unfailingly generous and he had been my friend for twenty years and I knew I should not have left him and his son at the airport and I felt

guilty and, suddenly, emotionally discombobu-
lated.

My Filofax contained a mess of numbers for
Sheridan, erasures, arrows leading down and up
like Snakes and Ladders. I rang them all, but never
got anything more encouraging than an answer
machine with Clara's voice on it. I then tried Jack
Ledoux but Jack's number was busy and I turned
my attention to Kelvin's fancy new espresso.

It was nine in the morning in Sydney and I was
jet-lagged and fuddled, and wrongly estimated
that it was midnight in Manhattan. I could see
my wife and children sleeping, hear their breath
like prayers whispering through the dark. By the
time I had the coffee in its elegant white cup I was
home and homesick all at once.

I should have got on the phone and talked to
the friends whose stories I wished to collect. I had
already categorised them as Earth and Air and
Fire and Water. All I had to do was call them but
instead I wandered through Kelvinator's paint-
perfumed house like a ghost, from light to dark,
from dark to light, from late-Victorian front door
to a café-modern kitchen whose steel-framed
glass doors looked over a black swimming pool.
It was hard not to be at least a little jealous. The
house itself was only thirty feet wide, but after
Manhattan the space seemed limitless. The hall-

way was generous, the ceilings high. The deep double front room had once been two rooms but now it was a big cold dining room – why did no one in Sydney ever heat their house? – and a library filled, mostly, with biographies and history books. I could find only one novel, *The Third Policeman* by Flann O'Brien.

This was a strange discovery in a house where no one read fiction, but when I opened the book Sheridan's handwriting appeared before me. Suddenly it was not strange at all. Sheridan always gave away novels, not only novels, but all sorts of writing, scraps of wisdom, useful facts, passages of beautiful prose. To Janet and Kel from Sheridan, I read, in memory of the silver wind. Silver like a knife. January 3 1996.

Sheridan had no respect for books as objects, writing in their margins, dog-earing their pages, interleaving them with his candy wrappers and socks and other unlikely bookmarks. But I never knew a man who had such faith in words, for he was always trying to give his friends that piece of jigsaw which would fit the gap, ease that ache that ignorance must surely be making in our hearts.

Page thirty-one of this first edition of *The Third Policeman* was dog-eared, and he had marked the following dialogue with a heavy ballpoint pen.

'No doubt you are aware the winds have colours,' he said. I thought he settled himself more restfully in his chair and changed his face till it looked a little bit benign.

'I never noticed it.'

'A record of this belief will be found in the literature of the ancient peoples. There are four winds and eight subwinds, each with its own colour. The wind from the east is a deep purple, from the south a shining silver . . .'

Why had Sherry marked this passage? It wasn't hard to figure out. He had signed his inscription on January 3, the high season of the southerly buster. My guess was that they had all just been crewing Meredith's boat on Pittwater. They had been hit by a deadly silver wind and something had broken or busted: they'd had some wild torquing adventure that popped the cabin furniture out of the floor. They were all cowboys, the women too. Kelvin's photo-editor wife was the wildest of them all.

Jack Ledoux sailed with them sometimes although he once intimated that they were too reckless for his taste. Tell me, Jack demanded, after Kelvin and Sheridan had shredded one more spinnaker in a Force 6, why are they always getting into trouble, Peter? And raised those eyebrows so high they disappeared beneath his dense white hair.

He's one to talk, said Sheridan. Christ, have you seen that little skiff of his? That's a man who wants to die.

And it was Jack Ledoux who had had the wildest experience with a Sydney southerly. He was in my notebook under Air. I had already phoned him from New York and he had tentatively agreed to tell it to my tape machine.

I tried his number again, and this time the phone was answered, so it seemed, by a screaming baby. It was a moment before I heard Jack's weary voice asking his caller to hold a mo.

I pictured my old friend inside his famous open-sided house beneath the sandstone cliffs of Pittwater and while I listened to the baby crying I remembered a night before his oldest boy was born when Kelvin and I had tried to load Jack up with all the baby stuff Kelvin had no use for any more. But Jack was fifty-six years old and had spent a life living the Life of Few Possessions and although we helped him pack the detritus of Fisher-Price and Babycare into his mouldy Saab, he brought it back again next morning.

Sorry, Kel, he said. I just can't do it.

But he could now. And did. Now he was a grey-haired former aesthete walking back towards the phone, travelling through a minefield of nappies and cribs and plastic toys.

I was just talking to Sheridan about you, he said. Just hung up.

Where is he?

Someplace *very* high, he laughed. He has some *vital* material for you to read. Jack laughed again. Actually, I'm pleased you called, because I've been thinking of that story of mine. I know I promised you . . .

God damn, I thought. He's backing out.

You know, Peter, I very nearly died. When something like that happens, when you've got off the hook, it's best to be very quiet, don't you reckon?

Off the hook?

Besides, he said a little sternly, there are those old privacy issues.

He was referring to something I do wish he would forget. Once I had taken a beautiful house he had designed and carelessly given it to a certain fictitious character, a man deeply involved in Sydney's corrupt world of business and politics.

I had intended nothing more than a tribute to a work of art, but I was thinking like a novelist not an architect and there is no doubt that Jack, a fastidious man, would never have built a house for this character of mine.

When he read the book he wrote me a very

27

angry letter. I had put his client's house, his private rooms, on public display. I had committed an utter breach of trust.

But was not this 'house' now fiction, embedded in a work of fiction? Would it not be read as fiction by everyone except those very few people who knew that a similar house really existed? All this I argued in my reply to him. I also said I was sorry and I meant it. It is easier to build imaginary houses than real friendships.

I have lived in more than one house Jack has designed and would be a happy man if I could wake up in one tomorrow morning and live in it all my life. Every time I walk into one of his constructions, it makes me happy. That being said, his notion of a house is a campsite. He likes it best when there are no walls at all, and his houses are made in the tension between his desire to be open to the elements and his clients' desire for protection from them. I remember leaping out of bed at three in the morning, manning the ropes, closing down the hatches as a storm lashed down out of the west. Jack Ledoux is a sailor, it shows in everything he does.

He is a very physical man, a natural athlete, and yet his shoulders have begun to hunch, a change that has certainly been caused by hours spent, arms folded across chest, chin in hand, standing before a painting, or a piece of land, watching the pink Pacific light illuminate a sandstone cliff, or the water at the end of a mangrove creek turn copper as the sun drops and the tide recedes. It is not only his long body but his face that has been re-formed by the act of seeing. He has a strong jaw and nose but the face is creased and eroded like soft stone. The eyes themselves are private, contained behind clamped-down slitted lids, but every line in that weathered face, like a line of magnetic force, bends towards the twin poles of the eyes.

He can see like no one else I know. If I could persuade him to make public the story of his fight with death, you would experience Sydney Air and Sydney Water. You would see the light on Broken Bay and the colour of the deadly wind.

Well, he said, in a tone that did not make me optimistic, there's no need to decide just yet.

He said he was coming down to the city, to visit a house he had recently completed for two clients, really wonderful people, Peter, the pair of them are just extraordinary. Perhaps he could pick me up. We would look at the house, and then we could come back up here to Pittwater. He could set me up a mosquito net and I could sleep out on the deck, 'on the possum trail'. We might catch a fish, hang out with him and Brigit and I could get reacquainted with his kids and meet the new baby. About the story I said nothing, but there was nothing that would take its place.

All right, he said, there's a ferry to Church Point in ten minutes. I'll be on it.

While Jack is catching his ferry from Taylors Bay, I should roughly lay out the topography of Sydney, which is distinguished not simply by its one famous harbour but three complicated invasions of Water into Earth. The harbour is the central and perhaps most spectacular of these, but Broken Bay, twenty miles to the north, and, to a lesser degree, Botany Bay, five miles to the south, share many of the topographical delights that Trollope extolled when he wrote of the harbour in 1872: I can say it is lovely but I cannot paint its loveliness. The sea runs up in various bay or coves, indenting the land all round the city so as to give a thousand different aspects to the water, – and not of water, broad unbroken and unrelieved, – but of water and then again of land. And you, the resident, – even though you be a lady not over strong, though you be a lady, if possible, not over young, – will find unless you choose your residence most unfortunately, that you have walks within your reach as deliciously beautiful as if you had packed all your things and travelled days and spent pounds to find them.

Today Jack Ledoux will travel from the north-ernmost incursion to the middle one. And although all my friends have begun to complain about the traffic, Jack will make this journey from the Church Point wharf to the city in no more than it might take to travel up the west side of Manhattan, from Greenwich Village to the George Washington Bridge. He will travel beside the dazzling blue waters of Pittwater, along the valley-floor road of Frenchs Forest. Meanwhile I am still browsing through *The Third Policeman*, where I discover, on page sixty-seven, one more annotation in Sheridan's impatient hand. WHO DOES THIS SOUND LIKE?!!!! he wrote beside the following reference to the character of the sage de Selby.

De Selby has some interesting things to say on the subject of houses. A row of houses he regards as a row of necessary evils. The softening of the human race he attributes to its progressive pre-dilection for interiors and waning in the art of going out and staying there.

(Jack, I thought.)

This in turn he sees as the result of the rise of such pursuits as reading, chess-playing, drinking, marriage and the like, few of which can be satisfactorily conducted in the open. Elsewhere he defines a house as 'a large coffin', a 'warren' and 'a box'. Evidently his main objection was the confinement of a roof and four walls.

I was laughing out loud as Flann O'Brien, writing in a gloomy Dublin winter, magically, exactly, uncannily, predicted Jack Ledoux's architectural approach to life in subtropical Sydney.

[De Selby] ascribed somewhat far-fetched therapeutic values – chiefly pulmonary – to certain structures of his own design which he called 'habitats', crude drawings of which may still be seen in the pages of the *Country Album*. These structures were of two kinds, roofless 'houses' and 'houses' without walls.

Then, or soon thereafter (as they say in police reports), there was a loud knocking on the door. I answered with *The Third Policeman* in my hand to meet . . . de Selby!

Ha! cried the genius, tapping my shirt pocket where I had imagined my mini tape recorder safely hidden. The report-ah!

I transfer the machine to my backpack, and no more was said about it. Then we were back in that humid musty Saab and twenty minutes later we arrived on the east coast of Australia confronting one more of Sydney's natural wonders, the vertiginous sandstone cliffs at the end of New South Head Road.

The walls of the city, said Jack.

Below us rolled the great Pacific Ocean whose tropical waters give Sydney its particular light, so different from the cold ocean light of my southern childhood. It is one of a hundred places you will find in Sydney which take your breath away, and I, familiar but disoriented, was in a state of constant amazement that any metropolis could be so blessed.

Yet behind our backs, on the other side of the narrow winding blacktop of Old South Head Road, was another reminder of Sydney which familiarity often blinds us to – on the walls of paradise stood a block of clumpish red-brick flats. You didn't need to even look at it. You could feel the dull blindness in your spine.

Who could build such a thing? It is not as if Sydneysiders did not love the natural beauty of their city. Indeed, we have been driving our visitors crazy for two centuries with demands that they admire it too. We have always been a maritime people, a city of sailors, swimmers, surfers. Our garages are cluttered with fishing rods, beach umbrellas, outboard motors, tents. Indeed, Jack's passion for the campsite is a Sydneysider's passion.

So who could have put THIS here? It would have been depressing in Brooklyn or Queens but here it seemed criminally *insane*.

In my imagination I saw the builder, a man who did not wish to look at where he was. He had made the windows small on purpose. He could not bear to confront all those terrifying miles of empty inhuman sea. He did not want to be here, on this sterile sandstone cliff. Deep in his psyche he was a denizen of the sandstone city described by Watkin Tench in 1790. By the time this reaches you, the young captain wrote, the fate of this settlement, and all it contains, will be decided. It is now more than two years since we landed here, and within less than a month of three since we left England. So cut off from all intercourse with the rest of mankind are we, that, subsequent to the month of August 1788, we know not of any transaction that has happened in Europe, and are no more assured of the welfare or existence of any of our friends than of what passes in the moon. It is by those only who have felt the anguish and distress of such a state that its miseries can be conceived . . . the dread of perishing by famine stares us in the face.

It is here, or near here, where many a Sydney life has ended, as unhappy men and women have jumped off the cliff at a place known as the Gap. The Gap draws them still, although the media remain silent rather than increase the place's magnetic hold on misery.

As for Jack, he could never allow himself to be negative for long, and although he showed appropriate disgust about the buildings behind us he was soon celebrating the beautiful cloud banks off the coast. He explained why the clouds were building, but something here had chilled my soul and I did not pay attention.

If Jack had been one to dwell on death and desolation he would not have built a house here. But he was one of life's celebrators and in this neighbourhood he had built one more extraordinary machine for living. Am I going to describe it? No way.

But here again – the campsite. The walls closed for the winter, evaporated in summer. It was an elegant and thoughtful space, and I will reveal not one more thing – well, perhaps just one: the roof could raise and tilt like a white wing. We stood, Jack, the owner, myself, and admired the clear perfect slit of ultramarine sky. My heart, I confess, was once again filled with envy.

The noise of an approaching helicopter did not annoy me. After all, I sleep with fire trucks and police sirens going past my house each night.

What are the helicopters up to? Jack asked.

Someone off the Gap.

He frowned. Oh dear. Does it happen often?

All the time, once or twice a week.

As we looked up the helicopter entered the parallelogram of sky framed by the lifted roof and the rammed-earth walls. And there it stayed, like a black invader inside a human cell.

Oh dear, said Jack.

He turned to me, passing his large hand across the stubble of his jaw. Why don't you call Sheridan?

While I dialled the first of Sheridan's many numbers, Jack stood with arms folded across his chest, staring at his ruined sky.

CHAPTER FOUR

THE TWO HOUSES ON Pittwater had stood side by side for many years, although to call Jack's old place a 'house' is to stretch the truth a little. It had once been a house, and it certainly had a good solid sandstone fireplace, but by the time Jack paid his $2,000 and took possession, the structure had collapsed into a heap amongst the wild lantana. Jack had propped up the walls on two sides and put a corrugated-iron roof on top. He had constructed a deck, and here, in a place commanding spectacular views of the estuary and the escarpment, he had erected a Japanese soaking tub and this he then connected to a little stove which served not only to heat the bathwater but to provide a campfire for his deft and tasty meals.

Somewhere very near by, in the middle of the

floor, there was a toilet, as disconcerting to some guests as the household habit of naked bathing in the hot tub beneath the frosty stars.

Through this extraordinary campsite, burgling possums and thieving kookaburras came and went, the kookaburras by day, the possums by night, and when August came and the westerly began to blow, Jack's carefully drawn plans would be lifted straight off his drawing desk and carried, soaring like sea eagles, out above the scrub.

Snuggling right next door, behind Jack's blind back wall, was a more conventional structure, a rectangular wide-verandahed house with a big sandstone chimney at its heart. Alison and I had once owned this house, together with Sheridan and Clara. This old place had not been perfect. It lost light too early in the afternoon and it was very cold in winter, but it had this splendid wide verandah on which great thick wistaria vines had twisted themselves.

It was to this site that I returned with Jack late that afternoon, walking up the steep path through the white-barked gum trees. As I walked I could feel the pressure of the tape recorder in my pocket, but there was an even greater pressure in my heart because both these houses had been violently destroyed.

In January 1994, when we were in our fourth year in New York City, fire swept down that hill, leaping with explosive force across the steep fire trail along which Alison and I had so often walked at the end of our day's work, a trail on which she had suggested I change my character 'Hermione' to 'Lucinda', a trail which led, not through this dreadful hell of burning birds and trees, but to a high rocky bluff where you could sit beside huge cinnamon-barked angophoras, their trunks as smooth as human skin, and look down to that cerulean blue water and above it the ultramarine sky and when I wrote, in those years, about being in love, then these trees and this water were part of the language together with, thwack, the tight tumescent smack of a spinnaker filling with wind on the water far below.

It was here that our first son had been conceived while the jacaranda petals lay upon the lawns like so many carelessly discarded jewels.

It was here that the fire roared like a train, incinerating our house, Jack's house, breakfast cereal, baby photos, fishing rods, mosquito nets, garden hose and a lifetime of Jack's plans, not only houses but big dreams for Sydney, a gateway topped by a dance floor above Circular Quay, an idea to turn Darling Harbour into 'lungs', a passageway for fresh salt air down into the forsaken edge of Broadway.

I am sorry, My Lord, to add to this letter, wrote John Hunter almost 200 years before, that we have this last summer experienced the weather so excessively sultry and dry that from the very parch state of the earth every strong wind has occasioned conflagrations of astonishing extent, from some of which much public and much private property has been destroyed. Some of the settlers have been ruined by losing the whole produce of their harvest after it had been stacked and secured; others have lost not only their crops, but their houses, barns, and a part of their livestock, by the sudden manner in which the fire reached and spread over their grounds. Trains of gunpowder could scarcely have been more rapid in communicating destruction, such was the dried and very combustible state of the vegetation, whether grass or tree.

In January 1994 all of Sydney seemed alight. The city was ringed with fire, ash fell in the Central Business District and it was not hard for my friends to imagine a ghastly apocalypse, petrol stations exploding the whole of white civilisation in flames. It was at about this time that people began to pay attention to Tim Flannery who was saying that the landscape which the white people found on arrival had been a carefully tended one, produced by a planned regime of burning, that practice known as 'firestick farming'. Commenting on John Hunter's letter, Flannery wrote: By now [June 10 1797] the Eora had experienced a decade of European interference. The effects of disease, farms and settlement meant that they were no longer able to manage their land by burning it as they had done for millennia. Death-dealing bushfires with their terrifying roar and unimaginable heat were becoming a major problem.

By the time I returned to Sydney in 2000 the whole issue of firestick farming had become particularly intense. Fire was defining not simply the landscape but the political climate and I would later have the slightly odd experience of sitting in an expensive Sydney restaurant, looking out across to the harbour and the opera house, and hearing two of my friends almost come to blows on the subject. Then I would see what a long way it was from New York.

But, for now, I walked in the slightly mournful light towards Jack's house, avoiding looking in the place where my old house had been.

There's fucking nothing there, mate, Sheridan had written to me. Nothing but the chimney in the middle of a lawn. I can't go there.

I also kept the chimney behind my back, although as I stepped up on top of the platform on which Jack's new house was built, I could feel the absence pressing between my shoulder blades. It was, alas, my way. I have a lifetime of turning my back on painful memories.

Jack's rebuilt house, being constructed in true de Selby fashion, still had no more walls than the previous model. Its one solid wall was blind and windowless, politely turning its back on its neighbour. Jack's place faced out towards the estuary, and thus, sitting in the steaming hot-tub, I was able to look down to the mangroves, up to the high darkening escarpment, but to have no visible reminder – if you can discount the silhouettes of dead trees on the clifftops – of all that had been lost in the fire.

But later, having shared a bottle of Dead Arm Shiraz with Jack and Brigit, I dressed and wandered out on to the lawn. The wine and the bath had made me mellow and, as I walked across the thick damp grass in my warm bare feet, I was not prepared for the surge of grief that now rose in my throat.

There we had lunched on the verandah beside the dense and fragile old wistaria the brevity of whose yearly splendour was sweet and painful like a Monet *Haystack*, arguing, in the moment of its greatest beauty, the shortness of our lives. There the black snake had lived beside the sandstone steps. There had lived and died an ancient Vietnamese palm. There were the remains of the water tank in which another snake had died, and there, still, was the careful terracing which the original builder, the director of a mental institution, had his inmates construct, free of charge, on his weekends.

With the red glow of fires all about them, Sheridan and Jack had stayed there one last night. They cooked a final meal, and at half past four in the morning, as the fire jumped the last break and spread in a great whoosh across the crowns of eucalypt, they boarded Jack's rowing boat, pulled off into the bay, and watched the houses burn.

Damn, said Sheridan. Fuck it. Damn.

CHAPTER FIVE

OF ALL THE WINDS that define this city, it is only
the westerly that I hate. It is a bullying blustering
wind and it blows for all of August and often for
October too. In 1984 a westerly wind came down
the Parramatta River at 100 miles an hour and
lifted the roof off my bedroom on Louisa Road. I
was not there to witness the bookshelves fall or
the sliding glass doors crash and break into
murderous daggers on my bed but my neighbour,
the shipwright Arthur Griffiths, saw the roof sail
across the street with its frilly Victorian lamp-
shade still hanging from the centre of its ceiling.
He saw it bounce off the house across the way
and land in the waters of Snails Bay.

Years later Jack Ledoux rebuilt that bedroom.
He devised a system of shutters so we could
batten down against the brutal westerly but,

being a follower of de Selby, he also worked to remove any barrier between the room and the world outside. The shutters and the windows all slid back and tucked away as if they were not there. The railing slid down too, so when the building inspector had left and when young Sam Carey was safely tucked in bed, there was no physical or visual separation between inside and outside.

What about mosquitoes? Even as I asked it I wondered if Jack really understood. He had always calmly coexisted with mosquitoes, ticks, leeches. (Fifteen years later, by the lantern light out on his deck, I would see Jack and Brigit's four year old bravely attack his own foreskin with a pair of tweezers.)

Well, said Jack, it would be criminal to put flywire over that.

Jack, I'm not paying all this money for mozzie bites.

Well, he said, why don't you talk to Brigit?

These days Brigit has a very successful practice but in those years she was Jack's former student, shockingly young, very pretty, and I thought her rather fey. But now she addressed 'the mosquito issue' and revealed the very practical aspect to her character. She made a stunning curtain. It was very fine royal-blue silk, Velcro'd on the sides, weighted at the bottom, and when I think of Louisa Road I remember, not that rude blustering bad-tempered westerly, but the sweet nor'-easter as Alison and I lay in bed and looked through the jacaranda to the water while Brigit's gossamer curtain just . . . breathed.

The room was a civilised abstraction of Jack's camp on Pittwater where, once the tick had been safely removed from the foreskin, we sat feasting on the crabs he and the kids had brought in from their trap.

You always hated the westerly, Jack laughed. So you tell the story of the lamp flying across the street, I'll tell you the story of the southerly, and we'll be square. But I think we should do it in the boat and I also think you should know what it's like to catch a kingfish. No book about Sydney is complete without a kingfish.

I slept with the tape recorder beneath my pillow, and when Jack shook me awake before dawn I tucked it in my trousers. It was dark and cold and we had drunk too much wine the night before and I followed Jack down the slippery dew-wet path to the mooring where he kept the skiff that had nearly killed him. It was slim and elegant and famously unstable. It was a working boat, with mast and sail and nets and fishing lines all lying open in the dark damp air.

Jack pulled the skiff in to the jetty and I got aboard. He threw me the handlines and squid then passed me the long oars and soon he was rowing through the pearly water in the direction of the pale dawn sky. Pittwater is a kind of paradise with its little coves, inlets, mangroves and the forests of glistening silver-trunked eucalyptus which come right down to the water. You could not look into this bush without imagining the past.

Men caught fish from the rocks, wrote Vincent Keith Smith, using long fishing spears with four or more hardwood prongs tipped and barbed with sharp fish and animal bones. Lying across their canoes with their faces below the water, they waited patiently . . . Women sat in canoes, fishing by hand with lines made of twisted strands of bark . . . the women talked, sang, laughed together as they fished, chewing mussels and cockles which they spat in to the water as a berley to attract fish.

Five minutes later, ten yards off the sandstone shore, Jack spilled tuna oil on to the water and, while we waited for those three green glistening kingfish which were presently nosing their way around the promontory towards their death, I finally produced my tape recorder, only to discover that the back panel had fallen off and one of the two batteries was missing.

Don't laugh, you bastard.

There was nothing malicious about Jack's laughter but as he threaded a squid on to the hook of his handline it was obvious just how relieved he was.

Anyway, he said, we'll get a kingfish.

He stood, balancing easily, and cast out a good fifteen yards to where the slick of tuna oil had not yet reached.

You could talk to Kelvin and Sheridan. Those fellows are always getting into strife. They'll tell you stories.

It's not the strife I'm interested in. The strife is just a way to show how the city is elemental.

Earth is an element, he said, seating himself on the aft thwart.

I know.

A friend of mine, Peter Myers, an architect, has written a wonderful paper called *The Three Cities of Sydney*. In fact he's going to deliver it this week at the university, and you really *must* hear him. He'll be happy to talk to you, I know he will.

I listened glumly. A university lecture was no replacement for a life-or-death struggle with the elements.

You knew the first settlers could find no limestone in Sydney, Jack said (and I was reminded, not for the first time, that he had been a famous teacher of architecture). And they needed lime if they were to make mortar.

They burned shells, I said resignedly. I know.

Yes, the first settlers extracted the *lime* for the mortar from *shells*. But what you might not know is that in 1788, when white people arrived, there were middens of shells *twelve metres tall* on Bennelong Point.

Where the opera house is.

Where the opera house is, exactly. Where Fort Macquarie was before that. So Bennelong Point was obviously the site of the first city of Sydney, and what an *ancient* city it was, do you see? There was a complex, very religious civilisation here when there were still Neanderthals alive in Europe, before the ice age ended and the oceans rose. This is the site of the most ancient civilisation on earth, but of course no one could see that in 1788. The convicts cannibalised the ancient city to make the colonial city. So the ancient city is still there, sandwiched between the bricks – baked earth – which contain, in turn, the thumb-prints of the men who made them. Twelve metres tall, Peter, can you imagine how many hundreds of thousands of wonderful feasts there were?

CHAPTER SIX

AT ABOUT THE TIME I hooked into my first ever kingfish, the English editor of *Granta* magazine was putting his 'Australia' edition to bed. In Hanover Yard, London, he wrote: Colonial history has nothing to be proud of here, but, considering Aborigines as a demographic statistic, the prominence of shame and intrigue about them . . . among the Australian intelligentsia is a remarkable thing.

Returning home I had been struck by the same thing. It seems obvious and yet it is not so simple an issue to grasp. If you look at it and see simple white liberal guilt you will be misreading the political landscape as confidently as the Europeans misread the physical land of 1788.

When I talked about the issue to Jayme Koszyn of the Brooklyn Academy of Music in New York, she asked me, how many Aboriginal people do you actually know?

One.

One?

There were only 700,000 Aboriginals living off this country when white people first arrived. Today there are 400,000 (in a population of 18 million) but you can live and die a white Sydneysider and never meet an Aboriginal. And yet we are obsessed, have always been obsessed, with the original inhabitants, even while we anticipated their passing, while we labelled them 'doomed', stole their land and children too.

Thinking to find an exact measure of this obsession, I searched through the Stanley Gibbons stamp catalogues in the New York public library. It was in its postage stamps, I figured, that a country represented itself to the world and my recollection of my childhood stamp album was that Australian postage stamps had been filled with Aboriginal portraits and motifs.

In the library I discovered that the 1930 two-penny stamp was exactly as I remembered it – the hunting Aboriginal. I also had picture-perfect recall of the two-shilling crocodile of 1939 and the Aboriginal of 1946. But that was it. What I had remembered was all there was to know. In all the years from Federation until 1955 there were no other depictions of indigenous people. There were many, many of George VI, Princess Elizabeth, Queen Elizabeth, Captain Cook, Matthew Flinders; there were dukes and duchesses and the Melbourne Cup – in short a portrait of a self-doubting corner of the British Empire.

You would think, to look at these stamps, not that we were obsessed, but we were forgetful of the facts. The Romans celebrated the barbarians they led away in chains, but not my ancestors.

As Kelvin had said so passionately, we had fought a war of occupation, at the same time pretending that the land was not used, barely inhabited.

Yet even the most racist amongst us must grant the Aboriginals intimate knowledge of this hostile land, and that is where they gain their authority in our imagination.

They knew how to live off this land, and we did not, and still do not. In report after report the first settlers described the fertility of the soils. (I find myself surrounded, wrote Francis Grosse, with gardens that flourish and produce fruit of every description.) This was madness. The soil was ancient, leached, sterile. When they saw parks, which they described repeatedly, they were seeing what they wished to see, a mirage of the deep soils that the ice age had bestowed on Europe.

Here there had been no glaciers to grind the rock to soil, and if there were only 700,000 people inhabiting the entire continent, it was because that was what the continent could sustain.

The term El Niño was not in the vocabulary of Governor Phillip when he set his motley crew ashore, but the meteorological pattern it labels had been in force for thousands of years and the land was subject then, as it is now, to erratic swings of weather, droughts, floods. It did not matter how you rendered it in oils, or how optimistically you described it in your letters home, this was not Europe, or America for that matter.

The truth is that Sydney Cove was only fit for blackfellows, or only blackfellows were fit for Sydney Cove. They did not need a ship to provision them, and if no ships had come from England for another 50,000 years a lot more of them would have survived.

Our white ancestors, by contrast, were left unprovisioned for just two years, and in that time their crops failed and then they lived with the terror of starvation. This story has been often told, and yet I wonder if we give full weight to the trauma of those years. The fact that there is no Thanksgiving in Australian culture is no small thing.

Many a guard, wrote Watkin Tench, have I seen mount in which the soldiers without shoes exceeded that which had yet preserved remnants of leather.

Nor, he continued, was another part of our domestic economy less whimsical. If a lucky man who had knocked down a dinner with his gun, or caught a fish by angling from the rocks, invited a neighbour to dine with him, the invitation always ran, 'Bring your own bread.' Even at the governor's table this custom was constantly observed. Every man when he sat down pulled his bread out of his pocket and laid it by his plate.

The insufficiency of our ration soon diminished our execution of labour. Both soldiers and convicts pleaded such a loss of strength as to find themselves unable to perform their accustomed tasks. The hours of public work were accordingly strengthened or, rather, every man was ordered to do as much as his strength would permit . . .

While Tench fretted, the indigenous people ate possum and snake and feasted on bunya seeds and a huge variety of wild food which the invaders would not touch to save their very lives. They did not learn either. A century later the explorer Burke died of starvation in a landscape where healthy families of Aboriginals were going about their daily business.

It is not romantic or wishful to say that the Aboriginal people made their religion from this earth and its conservation. Their stories grew from the land and were laced through the land and provided detailed instructions for the care of the land. Yet we know that, even when these stories are told to us, we are getting The Dummies' Guide. This is the condition of being a non-indigenous Australian; to know the land itself is like the index to a bible which we cannot read.

This then puts those who *can* read the stories in the role of priests and that is unbearably sentimental to outsiders (and many insiders too) but may further illuminate *Granta*'s opinion that Aboriginals provided 'an unpunishing version of Catholicism; the sacred suppliers of art, mystery, tourism, identity and guilt'.

There is another complication in the imagined dialogue between Us and Them. White Australia still has a strongly underdog culture, one that grew directly out of the experiences of transportation, exile. So even if the convicts raped and murdered blacks (which they certainly did) they also left for succeeding white generations a keen nose for injustice.

The peculiar history of Sydney has left us with

two sets of underdogs in the cultural dynamic. Judging our ancestors' behaviour with our ancestors' values, we find their behaviour abhorrent.

And if Jack and Sheridan and Kelvinator will, at every turn, consider where the Aboriginals walked, fished, burned, this is not simply romantic or even guilty talk, just white men finally learning about the country that they love.

CHAPTER SEVEN

UNRULY KELVIN DRAGGED THE chart away from
his friend Lester and carried it to the table by the
pool. The map showed the east coast of Australia
and Lester's extraordinarily neat recording of
their yacht's progress through the murderous
seas of the 1998 Sydney–Hobart race.

We followed the rhumb line, said Kelvinator.

No we bloody didn't, said Lester. The rhumb
line, he explained to me, is the direct line from
Sydney to Hobart, and that's where the flat-out
racers go, in the shallow water by the coast. It's
called rock-hopping.

Kelvin peered belligerently at the chart. I
thought we followed the rhumb line, he said.
But he stood back now and allowed his friend
to control the map.

Jesus, Kelvin, where were you?

On deck, Kelvin snorted, when I had to be. He uncorked a second bottle of Pinot Noir and filled our glasses.

Lester had come straight from his office in a dark Italian suit. It was hard to imagine him on any deck, but now he retrieved his chart and carefully placed his brimming wine glass to one side in order that he might unfold it to its full extent for me. His finger traced the grid of small neat numerals that I had always seen on charts but never understood.

These numbers represent fathoms, he said. A fathom is six feet. So you can see that the leaders in the '98 race hit the storm in three or four hundred feet of water while we were further east in fifteen thousand feet. That was my choice. I had been to the weather briefing the day before Christmas and what I saw there disturbed me.

The meteorological briefing took place on a hot bright Sydney morning. The water in Rushcutters Bay was mirror smooth, Force Zero on the Beaufort scale. The Cruising Yacht Club was chock-a-block. This is one of the rules of the race – the skipper and the navigator must attend the meteorological briefing which was given, in this case, by a certain Kenneth Blatt.

The clown was wearing a Santa Claus hat, Kelvin interrupted.

Yeah, well, that was sort of OK at the time but later the hat did make me angry.

No, Kelvin said, at the time too.

Lester hesitated. I was uneasy, yes, he admitted. Of course I had no clue of what was going to happen, but there was too much macho ho-hoing to my taste. Ken Blatt put on his red hat and his white pompom and said he'd run the various weather data through three or four different weather models and none of them could give him a coinciding view of what the weather systems were likely to be. So what he told us, in this jokey way, was . . . you're going to get hit by something somewhere.

To be fair, that's normal for the Hobart, said Kelvin.

To be fair, said Lester, five yachts sank, six men died.

Lester and Kelvin and eight other friends sailed from Neutral Bay at one pm on December 26 1998. It was not their boat. They were along as crew on Gordon Cameron's *White Lie 2*.

It was Saturday, a bright perfect summer's day in Sydney Harbour, and as *White Lie 2* made its way out towards the Heads there was information available in Hobart that showed a deepening low-pressure system 600 miles away in Bass Strait. They were all on deck here, even Lester who would soon retire to the navigation table where he would remain wedged for the next thirty-six hours.

We were about third last out the Heads, Kelvin laughed. You have a little spit when you come out the Heads. That's the custom.

He means a vomit.

Every time I've done it, said Kelvinator, I've had a spit but never again after that.

I've never had a spit, says Lester. Never. But I've seen Kelvinator eat half a plate of lamb navarin, throw it up, then finish the second half.

Only way.

It's nerves, says Kelvinator, not sea sickness. In 1998 there was a fair-sized swell, but it was nothing like the year before. Just on nightfall we had this ROLLING weather coming in on us in a straight line. In the middle of the night, there are about five of us around the sink, all vomiting in the dark. But it was just tension. You know there's at least a fifty per cent chance you're going to get clobbered. But you're really excited and all of us, except Lester who has gone down-stairs to sharpen his pencils, are on deck. This is a great time in any race. You've had your spit and it's just fabulous. You forget you are married. You forget you've got to fire your office manager and your shares are down the toilet. But about three or four hours out, the watch kicks in and now you get serious because you know you've got to race the boat. The wind is twenty-five knots. At this stage, with the spinnaker up, it is incredibly fast. It's the sort of sail you live for.

By eight o'clock, says Lester, we had travelled sixty-five miles and were due east of Nowra with the wind still behind us. That was when we got the first storm warning. Winds of forty-five to fifty knots south of Merimbula.

Merimbula, said Kelvin, is, comparatively speaking, sheltered. And you think, oh shit, if it's like that in Merimbula what will it be like when you poke your nose around the corner into Bass Strait? Now it's clear, we're definitely going to get clobbered, but what can we do? Turn around? Go home and say, ah, sorry, it was going to get rough? No, you're stuck like a train on rails. You're not only stuck, you're committed, you're CHARGING towards it flat out. And, Peter, honestly, the conditions were perfect. By nightfall we were as far as Jervis Bay, that's eighty miles in just eight hours, pretty good for a big heavy boat.

We took the spinnaker down before it got dark, said Lester.

Other crews might have been able to deal with a spinnaker in the night but it's fair to say, said Kelvinator, that we're more cautious. Some of these other boats, they train all year, the crew sleep out on the rails. But we're amateurs. We haven't done a lot of racing at night with spinnakers on.

If you get hit by a line squall . . .

It wraps around your mast.

Yendys had trouble with its spinnaker that night. They were bringing it down in thirty-eight knots.

Yeah, it broached, rolled on its side. These guys are pros but they lost their bowman off the side without a life jacket.

He wasn't hooked on. He . . .

Got washed clear off the boat and then a big wave dumped him back on the deck.

That was a lucky bugger.

That was a very lucky bugger.

That first night out, as *White Lie 2* hurtled down the coast, the crew worked their shifts but now Lester knew there was a storm ahead he would not leave the desk. He may have been one of the few navigators in the race who kept his radio on all the time.

I'm a control freak, said Lester proudly, wobbling his head as he always does when he speaks well about himself.

The one thing I don't like about sailing, said Kelvin, is going into the night. Going into the night with a storm coming is really a gut-churner because if you're going to die, you'd really like to die in the light. There's a whole lot of noise in the night, creaking stuff, and most of it is to do with stress, on wire . . .

A little boat will hurt you but a big boat will kill you. There are wires that can snap, spinnaker poles that can spear you right through the chest . . .

While *White Lie 2* carried my friends through Saturday night and the early hours of Sunday morning, a cool pool of air in Bass Strait was deepening into a low-pressure system. At first it was moving eastwards but then it slowed down and was cut off from the high winds that might have sent it safely on its way.

At three in the morning there was a sked, says Lester. That means that the navigator of every boat calls in his or her position, and they give us a forecast. There are two of these a day and they take an hour or more to get through every boat.

If the forecast had been a fish, said Kelvin, you would know enough never to eat it.

Well we didn't know that then, said Lester, but the forecast they gave us at three in the morning had been issued at nine o'clock the night before. What was forming ahead of us was actually a cyclone.

They don't call it a cyclone in these waters.

They call it a fucking storm.

At four in the morning of the second day, while we were off Narooma and Montague Island, it was snowing in Victoria. In midsummer. We had no idea.

By now the leaders were starting to get the serious weather from west-south-west. They still didn't know the extent of it, but we were in the lee of the mainland.

By the middle of the morning the low-pressure system was starting to pass directly over the racetrack and these terrifying winds and seas hit the shallows of Bass Strait. What you've got here is swirling cold eddy colliding with the warm East Coast current. This is horrendous – the waves collide and whip up Bass Strait until it feels like you're in a washing machine in hell.

I'd only been on Bass Strait once before, says Lester, and that was on a freebie on the *QE2* in 1986. And we had a Force 10 storm. The *QE2* had to throttle back from about thirty knots to twenty-five and I thought to myself . . . Fuck.

You would *not* want to be in a yacht in this sort of stuff. I went out on to the wing of the bridge deck in a pair of light cotton pants and the wind was blowing the hems of my pants so hard that it stripped all of the stitching out and the hems of my pants just dropped down. It was fucking horrible, but the wind that we were heading into was worse than that. Force 11.

Just after lunch, says Lester, I am on the nav table when I hear *Rager* report they're getting fifty to sixty knots with gusts up to seventy-two.

Then suddenly shit was happening everywhere, then *Team Jaguar* lost its mast . . .

Then a loose rope wrapped itself around *Team Jaguar*'s propeller. Jesus!

Our radio started going mad, said Lester. The news was devastating.

It was time to get battened down, said Kelvin, to look around the boat to see what will fall over, what will fall out of the shelving. We got the weatherboards across the hatchway. In a full storm you can't have any air down below because you can't let any water in. So it is dark and hot down there. You can't have much light on because you don't want to waste the juice. It's REALLY sweaty. You're dressed in thermal underwear that you will need on top. It's unbearably hot.

The whole environment is stinky.

Like most yachts, *White Lie 2* is not exactly waterproof so when the water washes across the deck a lot of it finds its way below. When the winds changed everything got very wet very fast. The cleanest and driest place to rest your head was on your hands.

The two o'clock sked ran for about an hour and a half. And listen to this, this is the forecast: a low centred east of Flinders Island will move to the east-south-east. West, west to south-west twenty-five to thirty knots (greater in gusts) increasing to thirty to forty knots offshore and forty to fifty near the Victorian coast. Swells one to two metres increasing to three metres. Waves two to three metres increasing to four to five.

We were only off Merimbula and we were getting seas as bad as that. While they were issuing this forecast *Stand Aside*, one of the leaders, submarines and rolls on a thirty-metre wave. One of the guys is washed off, sucked in, shot like a fucking cannon through the water.

I remember *Sword of Orion*, after they reported their position, they said, we don't know where that weather forecast came from. We're getting seventy and eighty knots here.

When you're on the table, you're really focused

on the work, but also this horror began coming out of the radio. Maydays, masts broken, boats rolling over, falling off the top of waves. What was it like, being locked between decks while all this was going on outside? It was frightening, because you don't really know what's going on upstairs. The boat makes some amazing noises. It's like being inside a hollow tin with some lunatic banging on it with a cricket bat. You can't brace yourself.

At four o'clock we changed course, heading south-east into even deeper water.

Soon the sky got very white, says Kelvin, and the tops were blowing off the waves and the air was filled with spume pelting at you horizontally, so hard it hurt, like hail. We had waterproof hoods but when we faced the sea the wind just peeled them off.

I don't know how big the waves were. We didn't have thirty metres, but it was big, and waves were coming from every direction. And the foam was dark, sort of grey, and the water had this weird sort of oil slick, like it had been emulsified. It was very unnatural and yet you're in the thick of it, and adrenalin driven, and there's not that much fear.

Later I would have a chance to observe Lester working on a yacht off Sydney. I learned things about his character I had never guessed in all the thirty years I'd known him. In the world of business he lacked the killer instinct, but in the face of a violent southerly he was fast and precise and calm and disciplined. This was someone you would want beside you in a war.

You can't let the fear take you over, said Lester, because you've got a job to do and that's the only thing that is going to get you out of there.

WORN-NIN, WORN-NIN. There was this idiot on the radio. He had this Kenneth Williams English accent. WORN-NIN. He sounded like he should have been behind the counter of a lolly shop.

Fuck off, idiot, said Lester. Worn-nin.

We had a shitload of food, a lot of food from Sheridan's wife, Clara, she's a chef as you know. We had bloody duck confit and Christ knows what else but we couldn't touch any of it, couldn't even get to it. In those storm conditions every movement is an exercise in callisthenics . . .

Even sitting at the nav desk is hard because you're flung in the chair from pillar to post.

I look at the chart again and admire Lester's neat annotations of hourly position. The only indication of anxiety is where, about this time, he annotates *White Lie 2*'s position every thirty minutes rather than every hour.

The three o'clock sked finished at about a quarter to five. We were, at that time, just south off Cape Howe which is almost into Bass Strait. That whole system was starting to spin through here. We were still heading for Hobart but twenty-eight boats had retired and, although it was the skipper's decision as to what we would do, we had our own views which we shared with each other in twos and threes. We had begun to fall into two groups, the Quitters and the Fools.

The thing about going back, said Kelvin, is that it can be more dangerous than going forward. It's easier to maintain control of your boat if you are not beam on to the weather and the seas. People died going back to Eden . . .

This place, just off Gabo Island, is famous for bad weather.

Famous for shipwrecks.

There has been enormous loss of life in these seas, said Lester. The first time Bass came round the cape in his whaleboat he was trapped here. He went ashore for nine days. Also, if you want to think about it, Peter, this water may be responsible for the settlement of Sydney because when Captain Cook came across this way from New Zealand he poked his nose into Bass Strait and saw one of these gales and he headed north and discovered Sydney.

He might have discovered the Strait.

He might have discovered Melbourne, said Lester. Where the soil is actually much better.

By the time five o'clock came it was a shitfight. On the radio you could hear that people were dying. Lew Carter was the voice on the radio-relay ship. He was the hero. He was so cool. He would say to someone whose boat was sinking, could you hold there please while I take this other call and I'll come back to you as soon as I can. He never lost it.

I was firmly of the opinion, says Lester, that we should turn around. I wanted to get out of there.

I wanted to hang on a bit, said Kelvin. You see, we pulled out of the race the year before and now I know we quit too easily. That time we had big seas but we also had the headsail jammed in its track. It was ripped to shreds and we couldn't get it down and we couldn't get a new sail up. Now, there were two fellows up that mast and they both said it was jammed in the foil of the forestay, and I never thought to doubt them. But when we got back into Eden one of the blokes went to the bow and gave the sail a bit of a tug, and *WHOOSH* the remnants fell right down to the deck.

See, Peter, there's a window there when you make these decisions. Fear is rampant and it seems the logical thing to turn around but you have to push a bit further than that to get there.

But then, a minute later, Kelvin seemed to contradict himself. I remember, he said thoughtfully, when Gordon, our skipper, finally asked the crew's opinion. He and I were both looking out the long porthole, and he saw the same thing I did. This monster wave hit us WHACK. It was like being slapped by God. It was like being hit by a rock. The sea was showing us what it could do and it was prepared to show you more if you were not persuaded.

But Kelvin voted to go on.

We would have been all right.

We would have been fine, agreed Lester, in twenty-twenty hindsight. Now, having seen the satellite streaming video, I think it would have been better to go on. We probably put ourselves at greater risk by turning round. We had waves coming from behind us rather than taking them on the quarter. But I'm here. I feel no regret, believe me.

Kelvin said, I wasn't afraid until I got off the boat and saw the seas on TV in Eden. Janet came into the room and she said my jaw was wide open. Jesus, I could have been killed.

CHAPTER EIGHT

I HAD BEEN AT home in New York on the eve of
the millennium celebrations and at seven forty-
five on that Friday morning, while my wife and
sons were still sleeping, I ran quietly down the
stairs to witness my other home enter the year
2000.

Distracted by a man in the street who was
angrily eviscerating our household garbage, I
almost missed it, but at eight o'clock New York
time I finally turned to NBC where I saw the
opera house, the harbour bridge. Then Sydney
passed into the next century and the bridge
suddenly exploded.

Few cities in the turning globe would equal
that display at millennium's end, and yet I, the
sentimental expatriate, was less than enchanted
and my emotion suddenly cooled. I'd seen this

trick before. These fireworks were very similar to the display at our bicentenary in 1988. Then too the bridge grew green and fiery hair. OH WHAT A PARTY the *Sydney Morning Herald* had written then, and it had been true, the whole town was pissed. We had a classic Sydney rort and we disgraced ourselves with our total forgetfulness of what exactly it was that had occurred in this sandstone basin just two centuries before.

In the heat of our bicentennial celebration, the 50,000 years that had preceded the arrival of the First Fleet somehow slipped our minds. All right, it's a white-settler culture. It's what you might have expected, but that does not explain why we forgot the white people too, or most of them. In 1988 we commemorated the soldiers, but the men and women beneath the decks just somehow were overlooked in all the excitement. The twin forces of our history, those two cruel vectors which shape us to this very day, had been forgotten and what we celebrated instead was some imperial and bureaucratic past towards which we felt neither affection nor connection.

Twelve years later I stared balefully at the fiery bridge but as the smoke cleared I spotted an unexpected sign. Just a little to the left of the northern pylon, just near the place where my dare-devil friend G. had risen above the level of the roadway as he crawled upwards, like a worm in an apple, *inside* the hollow boxed girders of the bridge's arch, just there, a three-foot-high word was written in an illuminated copperplate:

$$\mathcal{E}\textit{ternity}$$

Seeing this, all my spleen was completely washed away, and I was smiling, insanely proud and happy at this secret message from my home, happier still because no one in New York, no one but a Sydneysider, could hope to crack this code, now beamed through space like a message from Tralfamador. What fucked-up Irish things it finally meant to me, I will struggle with later, but I cannot even begin to imagine what it might mean to a New Yorker.

An Aussie brandname? Something to do with time? Something to do with the millennium? Something, perhaps, to do with those 50,000 years of culture that this city is built on top of? But although 50,000 years is a very long time, it is not an eternity, and it is not why the people of Sydney love this word, or why the artist Martin Sharp has spent a lifetime painting and repainting it.

Martin is famous in Sydney, and like most painters his reputation is more local than international. If you live in Sydney you know he is obsessed with a 1930s funfair (Luna Park), a strange campy singer (Tiny Tim) and a word (Eternity). But if you are from somewhere else it may mean something that Martin Sharp wrote the lyrics for 'Tales of Brave Ulysses' which he gave to Eric Clapton in a pub one afternoon.

The secret of Eternity does not belong to Martin but he has been one of its custodians and I was determined to talk to him about it.

Kelvin groaned when he heard what I planned to do.

Mate, you're making a big mistake talking to all these men. You're ignoring the women. Listening to you, it's as if they don't exist.

I thought this was pretty rich, coming from a guy who calls his female crew members 'slotted personnel'.

My novels are filled with women, I said.

But no one reads novels, Peter. The world has changed, in case you haven't noticed.

Everyone is reading *Vogue* and *Elle*?

You're going to take a lot of shit for this, he said, and don't forget I warned you.

This exasperating argument continued and it was two hours before I was able to visit Martin. I found him, at midday, wandering, a little shakily, around his dusty inheritance, his mansion. His assistant had not yet arrived and he was trying to 'organise' a cup of tea. The man who designed Cream's album covers for *Wheels of Fire* and *Disraeli Gears* looked all of sixty when I saw him, hungover, with his handsome face unshaved, and creased with a classic smoker's skin. But I am of an age myself, and if I noticed the creases, I noted with envy that his hair, though greying, was thick and strong.

I first saw Eternity when I was a kid, he told me as he rolled his second cigarette. I came out of my house and discovered this chalk calligraphy on the footpath. No one ever wrote anything on the streets in those days. I thought, what's *that*? I didn't think about what it meant. I didn't analyse it. It was just beautiful and mysterious.

For years and years no one knew who wrote this word, said Martin. It would just spring up overnight. We now know the writer's name was Arthur Stace. We know he was a very little bloke, just five foot three inches tall, with wispy white hair and he went off to the First World War as a stretcher-bearer. Later he was a 'cockatoo', a look-out for his sisters who ran a brothel. Then he became an alcoholic. By the 1930s, when he walked into a church in Pyrmont, he was drinking methylated spirits.

The church had a sign offering rock cakes and tea for the down and out.

Well, Arthur went in for the cakes but he found himself kneeling down and joining in the prayers. That is how he gave up the grog and got 'saved' but the God-given task of his life would be granted to him at another church, the Baptist Tabernacle on Burton Street in Darlinghurst.

On the day Arthur came into the Tabernacle the Reverend John Ridley had chosen Isaiah 57:15 as his text. For thus sayeth the high and lofty One who inhabiteth eternity, whose name is Holy: I dwell in the high and holy place with him also that is of a contrite and humble spirit, to revive the spirit of the humble, and to revive the heart of the contrite ones.

Eternity, the preacher said, I would like to shout the word Eternity through the streets of Sydney.

And that was it, said Martin. Arthur's brain just went BANG. He staggered out of the church in tears. In the street he reached in his pocket and there he found a piece of chalk. Who knows how it got there? He knelt, and wrote Eternity on the footpath.

According to the story, he could hardly write his own name until this moment, but now he found his hand forming this perfect copperplate.

That was sign enough. And from then on he would go wherever he felt God call him. He wrote his message as much as fifty times a day; in Martin Place, in Parramatta, all over Sydney people would come out on to their street and there it would be: Eternity. Arthur didn't like the concrete footpaths because the chalk did not show up so well. His favourite place was Kings Cross where the pavements were black.

Actually, God did not always send Arthur to write on the footpaths. Once, for instance, He instructed him to write Eternity inside the bell at the GPO although, Martin Sharp told me, the dark forces may have tried to rub it out since then. Of course he didn't have permission. Arthur always felt he had permission 'from a higher force'.

I didn't have anything directly to do with that word appearing on the bridge, said Martin, but I have kept it alive; I suppose you could say that I have continued Arthur's work. The paintings you know, but I have also just finished a tapestry of Eternity for the library in Sydney. I'm pleased Arthur's work is finally in a library. He was our greatest writer. He said it all, in just one word. Of course he would be amazed to find himself in a library. And imagine, Peter, imagine what he would have felt, on that first day in Darlinghurst, to think that this copperplate he was miraculously forming on the footpath would not only be famous in the streets of Sydney but beamed out into space and sent all around the world.

I stayed with Martin talking for a long time, but we said no more about Arthur Stace. So it was not until much later that night, sleepless above Kelvin's garage, that I attempted to pin down the appeal of his message, not to Martin whose fascination with the word seems both spiritual and hermetic, but to the less mystical more utilitarian people of Sydney.

You might think this no great puzzle. But it is a puzzle – we generally do not like religion in this town, are hostile to *God-botherers* and *wowsers* and *bible-bashers*. We could not like Arthur because he was 'saved', hell no! We like him because he was a cockatoo outside the brothel, because he was drunk, a ratbag, an outcast. He was his own man, a slave to no one on this earth.

Thus, quietly reflecting on what might be the idiosyncratic, very local nature of our feelings for Eternity, I began to follow the vein back to its source until, like someone who dreams the same bad dream each night, 200 years just vanished like sand between my fingers and I was seeing Arthur Stace as one more poor wretch transported to Botany Bay.

And what might Eternity mean in such a place of punishment?

Eternity! O, dread and dire word, wrote James Joyce in that famous hellfire sermon in A *Portrait of the Artist as a Young Man*. Eternity! What mind of man can understand it?

It is a terrifying exposition of hell and I tried to escape it, to find some more pleasant place for my mind to rest. Typically I imagined the ocean but this Australian ocean was no escape. It was endless, relentless, merciless, and it washed against the sandstone cliffs out at the end of Old South Head Road. I thought of helicopters, cars driven off the cliff beside the British Council. And of course Joyce's sermon is filled, if not with sandstone, then with sand; as he tries to compute eternity he evokes the horror of a mountain of that sand, a million miles high, reaching from the earth to the farthest heavens, and a million miles broad.

Eternity Eternity Eternity.

In Woollahra at two am, looking out across Kelvinator's dirty swimming pool, I was seized by a sort of existential terror which it took a half bottle of Laphroaig to assuage.

CHAPTER NINE

WHEN I FIRST CAME to live in Sydney I daily drove from Wharf Road to North Sydney in my Jensen Healey. I careened across the harbour bridge at reckless speed, hood down, hair whipping my face. From May 1974 until January 1975, the bridge was no more than a road to me. But then, without warning, it became a source of terror.

One muggy January morning I drove to work as normal. That night I found I could not return across the bridge, although return I must for I was already in the middle of the centre roadway with trucks to left and right of me and all that great weight of dizzy steel above my head. It was seven o'clock and the traffic heading south was fast and relentless. And here some alien panic took me, rushing through me in a great hot wave, chemical terror, administered direct into my blood. Confused, I braked, accelerated, closed my eyes, drove in a jerky fright, certain that I would cross the centre line and hit a truck. I was unbearably giddy, irrationally terrified of the fall to the water, but also the vertiginous height of the arch above me.

When I finally descended to the Cahill Express-way I was a mess of sweat and shame, but I had little idea of what had happened to me. I certainly did not guess that a second bridge, a minuscule replica of the first, had been formed inside my brain and there it locked fast in place never to be undone, a fast and easy pathway to a previously inaccessible shore of panic.

Why this occurred does not really matter, although it was the opinion of the New York psychologist Arthur Fensterheim that the root cause was, as is so often the case he said, nothing more profound than too much coffee.

When, twenty-five years after this incident, I returned home with the martial-arts team, I had conveniently forgotten that the bridge was my Berlin Wall and that I would not drive myself across it to visit Jack Ledoux. Yet on the night I drank my half bottle of Laphroaig, I dreamed that I climbed the bridge, that I conquered it at last.

In my dream I leap halfway up the Cyclone

security fence around the southern pylon at Dawes Point, named for Lieutenant Dawes who had tried to learn the language (*Why are the black men angry?*). For a moment I cling spread-eagled on the wire, and then I swiftly pull myself up to the top. As in life, the security lights in my dream are quartz white. They wash across the face of the pylons, magnets for countless insects which now rise in dense clouds in the warm night air. The insects in turn attract gulls which spiral above my head, their white plumage shining in the dark. I feel, as I cleverly straddle the razor wire, as I drop lightly to the enclosed square of long dew-wet grass, that all of Sydney can see me. But it is three in the morning and the legal part of Sydney is sound asleep and the end of the lower arch, a great open box girder, waits for me as enticing as a rabbit hole in a child's story and I scurry on hands and knees from brightness into the safety of the dark.

I am inside the bottom arch of the bridge. I can stand upright. I am laughing, elated, but my heart is also beating fast and I wait a moment to calm down, short intakes, long exhalations, just as Dr Fensterheim taught me.

I need a torch and I have one, a heavy long job such as you buy, in the US anyway, from those mail-order catalogues containing instructions on garrotting and knife-fighting and other useful arts.

All in all, says the voice, that's a useful object.

In my dream I recognise him immediately – the narrator from *The Third Policeman*, the person who begins his narrative thus: Not everybody knows how I killed old Phillip Mathers, smashing his jaw in with my spade; but first it is better to speak of my friendship with John Divney because it was he who first knocked old Mathers down by giving him a great blow in the neck with a special bicycle-pump which he manufactured himself out of a hollow iron bar.

In short, a character you would be wise to be very careful of.

I make some non-committal response to his observation, but at the same time I am confused as to whether he means to say that the torch is 'useful' as a weapon and if I am being challenged to use it against him. I shine the light inside the bridge as if I make this journey every day. I find my view impeded, ten feet in, by a steel plate.

Ah, says my invisible companion, but there is a dirty great hole in the middle of it.

Indeed there is, and soon I am crawling through it. And then what do I find? Why, six feet ahead, there is a second metal plate, a second hole. So this is how it is going to be. My passage to the apex will be through a series of rooms, of steel boxes of gradually diminishing size. The height of these boxes is around seven feet when I set out but soon enough I need to stoop to accommodate myself to the engineer's will. This might be expected to produce resistance, then claustrophobia, but although it is increasingly clammy and hot and there is a musty raggy smell which reminds me of old Bertie Booker who cleaned cars in my father's GM dealership, the containment is unexpectedly comforting. I am the worm in the bridge's spine, the enemy it cannot see. I rise inside the arch unseen by all the world.

If you think to escape the terror, says the voice, then you are seriously mistaken.

I turn sharply towards him and knock my head so hard I drop the torch. It lands with a dreadful clatter but, thank God, is prevented from rolling far by the steel plate.

As I continue, the box beam narrows and I know I previously claimed that I had been comforted by the containment, but as I now come level with the roadway and feel the merciless roar of traffic, I drink deep on a whole cocktail of anxieties. Claustrophobia and vertigo flutter like possibilities around the penumbra of my consciousness. But I do not give in. My body is shaken by the traffic, nothing more.

I had never previously noticed quite how much the arches of the bridge slim as they reach the apex, but the bridge is a structure I have spent a lot of time avoiding. I never knew, for instance, that it is constructed as a mighty hinge, or two hinges bolted together at the apex. I certainly did not know that Jack Ledoux himself had passed along this very route.

I leave the roadway well beneath me and, if it is hotter inside the beam now, it is also quieter. As I approach the apex of the lower arch the white light of my murderous torch is well ahead of me, seeking the two large wing nuts I know to expect above my head. And there they are, one and a half inches in diameter, but fragrant with WD-40 and as effortlessly turned as spinning tops.

Ah, this next bit will test you, boyo.

But I easily push the steel trapdoor aside and lift my eager face into the sky.

The air tastes of rock oysters and I watch with a kind of ecstasy as a great train of white cloud scuds across the heavens.

You are thinking of Van Gogh, the narrator offers. It is *Starry Night* you're seeing.

I admit this is so.

There's madness, he says, that's insanity for you.

I am now at the apex of the lower arch and to

reach the upper arch I must climb this stairway which is but three feet from my hand. Foolishly I clamber on to the wide flat section of the arch. I try not to look at anything but the stairway which has been built by some cruel surrealist rising upwards in the middle of the wind.

Now, I cannot deny it, I am afraid. I tell myself it is just a dream and I grasp the two-foot-wide rungs of the ladder and lift my now leaden sneakers up through the nor'-easterly, ascending through three landings to the top arch of the bridge, and there I find my old friend Panic has been waiting for me all the time.

It is just a dream, but now I am whimpering like a child, shutting my eyes, lowering myself flat on to the slippery dew-wet bridge. I try to per-form those long J-shaped breaths that Arthur Fensterheim taught me but I am pinned, like a live butterfly fluttering on a board of steel.

And there I stay, for how long I cannot say except that in my dream I fall asleep and dream, and in this dream within the dream I cunningly manage to create my own escape. Through this ruse I am able to actually stand, and stretch, and look down from the bridge, and look out across the small fortified island of Pinchgut. But no sooner have I stood than Flann O'Brien's man is pestering me once again.

Peter Carey

Jesus help me, what's that?

I make no answer.

Might a man not ask a civil question? What's that flapping in the breeze down there? Answer me.

It must be Francis Morgan, I admitted.

Who in Christ's name is Francis Morgan?

Governor Phillip had him hung in chains until he rotted and fell into the sea.

And what's that blue plastic?

They're building a restaurant.

My God, that hanging chap would kill the appetite.

I gaze pointedly away from him, surveying first the Heads, the mighty incisors that protect the port of Sydney, then the ridges to the north where I can now see the headlights of a single car moving along Military Road, so called because it is the military highway to the batteries down which at Eastertide, with drums beating, colours flying, go the gallant guards of the city and colony.

The gallant guards of the city and colony. That's a quote.

In so saying he reveals that he can read my mind. It is from *A Traveller's Tale*, I confess. *From Manly to the Hawkesbury*.

Is not that hanging fellow making you giddy?

But I cannot see the hanging man and I am not giddy in the least. The bridge, it seems, is finally conquered. Now Sydney can be really mine. Now I actually dare to look calmly down into the quay where I can hear the comforting squeak and groan of the big steel ferries protesting their moorings.

And there, sweeping above and behind the ferries, a single motor-cycle comes off the bridge and sweeps down the Cahill Expressway.

Down there is the birthplace of modern Australia, although you would not know it. The expressway is like a steel wall, cutting water off from earth, slicing like a knife across the moment of our birth. Further back, in the midst of all that very ordinary architecture, is the towering building at Australia Square, beneath which runs the Tank Stream, which was our nation's breast, at which our founding fathers and mothers, jailers and jailed, all drank side by side. Now, of course, the Tank Stream is buried, a sandstone drain which will take a week of phone calls to get access to and where, in the freshly disinfected air, cockroaches flee before your light.

Above my head the clouds are racing, but I am in a sort of ecstasy where everything means something and I am awash with the giddy thrilling feelings that must come to schizophrenics

when all the secrets of eternity are suddenly laid
bare.

Read the signs to me, my companion demands.

Staring down into the Central Business District, I see the street signs have begun to burn like
glow-worms in the velvet night.

Phillip Street, I offer.

And who was that?

Our first governor, a naval officer.

Hunter Street?

After the foolish second governor, a naval
officer.

King Street? Not the damn King of England?

No. Another naval officer.

Bligh Street. This cannot be the same bastard
who drove his poor crew to mutiny?

Yes, the Colonial Office appointed him governor. He was recommended by Sir Joseph Banks
in fact.

Why would you celebrate a tyrant with a street
name?

Oh, we rose against him, I said.

Ah, at last some heroes. It takes great courage
to go against a bastard like that. Were the rebels
hung for it? What were the names of the martyrs?
Which streets are theirs?

The leader was a Captain John Macarthur.
The event was called the Rum Rebellion.

Macarthur? That is not a name I see. There is a
lot of arse-licking: Kent and Bathurst and Goulburn and Sussex and York and Pitt and George.
But where is Macarthur?

Well, Macarthur is a complicated figure for us.
He's a hard one to embrace. He was a Tory.

But did he get rid of the bastard Bligh or did he
not? Was he not a brave man?

Yes, very brave, and headstrong, but he was in
no way democratic. His notion of a parliament
would be four cronies and himself in charge. The
only convicts he had time for were those that
worked as slaves for him. He lined his own
pockets. He was an army officer but he used
his privilege to get rich. He and his officer mates
controlled the rum.

Ah, so a man who will not share a drink.

It was a monopoly the soldiers had for themselves. It was like being in charge of the mint.
This was a place where a man would work for
grog when he gave not a damn about the lash. If
you earned twenty shillings you would be paid a
pint of grog instead.

Wait a minute. Is this the same Macarthur who
is called the father of the Australian wool industry?

The very same man.

And is wool not the business that made the

colony feasible? Should you not acknowledge him in some way? A Tory, yes, but is he not worth more to you than Kent and Sussex? Should you not have a monument to him at least?

And then, in my dream, I peered down from the top arch of the Sydney Harbour Bridge, and had the insight which would never leave me, not even in my waking hours. Asleep in my bed in Woollahra I saw the Central Business District as if for the first time. I saw how it held itself back from the edge of the beloved harbour as if it understood how vile and crooked it had always been. In a society which values the view above all else, here was the heart of the city, a blind place with no vistas, a dense knot of development and politics and business and law. This was Macarthur's monument. A physical expression of two centuries of Sydney's own brand of capitalism, the concrete symbol of an unhealthy anti-democratic alliance between business and those authorities which should have controlled it.

Staring in horror at this ugly thing that we had made, I heard a pitiless grinding noise, some infernal machine, some engine of gears and chains, grinding very, very slow.

Come on, come on, the voice called, you can't let down your mates.

Far beneath me I heard Kelvinator's garage

roller door growling on its axis. It was six am in Woollahra. Time to drive to Bondi Beach to take our morning walk.

I stumbled in the dark and as I heard Kelvinator start the engine of his Jaguar I was very grateful to feel the floor beneath my feet.

CHAPTER TEN

TEN MINUTES AFTER THE grinding door had rescued me from this satanic vision of the CBD I was walking with Lester and Kelvinator and his mad brown kelpie along the firm yellow sand of Bondi Beach. In all the world, what metropolitan beach could equal this? Rio? I've never been there. Venice? Santa Monica? Don't make me laugh. This was the great joy of Sydney, that you could have THIS, the embracing yellow cliffs, the breakers long and slow, the texture of the Pacific like a polished Cadillac, a gorgeous eggshell blue with pink showing in the froth of the breaking waves.

This is what my Sydney friends could do each morning. They were never blind to where they were but they never stopped bantering, heckling, joking. On this particular morning they affected to be astounded that I had not yet got Jack Ledoux's story from him.

Jesus, *we* gave, said Lester, his voice rising in that self-mocking plaintive tone which was so characteristic of him. We gave our story, miss.

We bloody gave the damn storm of the century.

Kelvin and Lester had been taking these walks together so long, they had become like a pair of high-speed cockatoos, their brisk steps punctuated by familiar patterns of call and response. Pedant, pe-dant, fucking's too good for him. Worn-nin, worn-nin.

What sort of reporter are you anyway? Door-stop him.

Door-stop?

Put your bloody foot inside his bloody door and refuse to leave until he tells his story.

Jack doesn't have a door. In any case, I never saw him do anything he didn't want to.

And I never saw you *not* do something you wanted to do. Go. Take the car. Why do you never use my car? Does it smell or something?

I could have told Kelvin I had panic attacks on the bridge, but instead I changed the subject to something more congenial – my fantasy that Alison and I would sell the apartment in New York and come back home to live.

So I couldn't drive across the bridge. All I wanted was to bring our kids to Bondi Beach, to have a dog, to eat oysters at Hugo's over on Campbell Parade. I wanted us all to feel what it is like to live in a city with diminished population pressure.

What you actually want, says Kelvinator, is something two or three streets back.

There was a pleasant nor'-easter ruffling our shirts, a silky seductive wind, not strong but sufficient to disperse that dream of the knotted power and corruption of the Central Business District.

Could I get a house and garage and a pool and four bedrooms?

The Aussie dollar's worth fifty-six cents.

With US dollars, you'd piss it in said Lester.

In New York we cram a family of four into two small bedrooms. Alison and I work in offices the size of telephone booths. On Bondi I feel the space everywhere, not just in the luxury of beach and light but in that imagined house two streets back where I will not have to throw a book away to make room for each new one that comes in the door.

We are now following Kelvinator's sniffing pissing licky brown kelpie up the steps to the road that passes the Bondi Returned Services

League, a typically Bondi institution of the old
school. Barracks architecture, no airs, no charm,
but a fabulous view right out across the glassy
Pacific Ocean. This has been the mark of Bondi
always, the combination of immense natural
beauty and an unaesthetic but democratic spirit.
The rich stayed huddled inside the harbour or
drove up the coast to Palm Beach, but here on
Bondi you mix it with the hoi polloi. Or did.

If you're thinking about buying, said Kelvinator, dragging his ridiculously excited dog back
off the road, you better do it now. See that
building there, Packer paid two mill for one of
those apartments.

They reckon Packer is trying to buy the rissole,
says Lester. A rissole, in case you are from across
the sea, is a kind of hamburger patty, but it is also
an arsehole and also an RSL.

If he wants it, says Lester, he'll get it.

We three pause to look down on to the ocean
pool beneath the RSL. The pool, while having
nothing but a geographical connection with the
RSL, is of the same spirit. It is a public pool, a
democratic pool, rough at the edges, frequented
by all sorts of people, amongst them leather-
skinned sixty year olds in Speedo trunks and
faces like last winter's potatoes. Even the dog
stops licking to watch the waves crash over the

wall, cascade off the edge, foaming and spilling on the rocks beneath. The force of the ocean gives it an exciting, vaguely dangerous air. The impression is not exactly false. Can you see that enormous rock just off Ben Buckler, the northern headland of Bondi Beach? It was not there on July 14 1912. Next day it was delivered to the beach like a piece of flotsam. It weighs 235 tons.

They say the pool has concrete cancer. It'll take millions to replace. If someone doesn't buy it, it'll crumble into the sea.

This place is a Sydney institution.

Well, it is, says Lester, but if Kerry Packer wants it, then Kerry Packer will get it.

But the dog is off and we are after him, walking briskly round that clifftop walk that comes down into Tamarama Beach. Can Rio match this? The high sandstone cliffs? The intimate bays? The never-ceasing unfolding of beaches tumbling south, Tamarama, Bronte, Clovelly Coogee, so many of them that not only have the rich not bothered to claim the territory, but the dead have been allocated acres of absolute ocean front. The dead in Waverley Cemetery have the best views in the world.

But this is one of the distinctive features of Sydney, that there are so many miles of harbour, so many miles of coast, that the normal pressures for space are far less, and so places like the Waverley Cemetery and the Bondi RSL will survive, if not for ever, then longer than you might expect.

We retrace our steps along the clifftops and when we come back above the sand of Bondi a small crowd has gathered and TV news vans are arriving.

It's a protest, said Lester. They're building the beach volley-ball stadium here.

Here? They're putting it here? For the Olympics? I was astounded. How could they put it here, in the middle of Bondi?

You could always join the protest, said Kelvinator. Look at the crowd. There are at least twenty-eight people who agree with you.

And what do you think? I asked my friend.

They're losers! he giggled.

The jocks are in charge, explained Lester.

It was a shocking thought that a city could have so little appreciation of this place that they would desecrate it at a time it was to have its biggest influx of visitors.

It can't be stopped?

Not a chance, said Kelvinator. All twenty-eight of them can bury themselves in the sand up to their eyes and no one will change this venue. The jocks are in control. The fix is in, mate. The deal is done.

I would revisit Sydney in October. The Olympics were finally over but everyone was still chuffed, high as kites, over the moon, pleased as Punch, jocks and non-jocks, just exhilarated by the experience of the Games. Nothing else had been done in Sydney for those two weeks. People went to the Games or stayed at home and watched TV. They stopped shopping. Retail sales dropped 20 per cent. Intellectuals who had been sour and cynical in April had changed their minds completely and even those who had felt as I did about the beach volley ball would tell me, Peter, it was not so bad. It's all gone now. The beach is back to normal.

In the great wash of pride that the Games left in their wake my friends seemed inclined to forget the continual scandals that had marked the years before the Games began.

It's what you expect, said Lester.

Yes, there was corruption, Kelvin joked, but it paid off.

There were so many episodes one could choose to illustrate the Sydney way of doing business, but the most breathtaking involved Kevan Gosper, once a famous athlete, now the vice president of the International Olympic Committee.

Until this particular scandal broke all Australia

knew that a fifteen-year-old Sydney girl named Yianna Souleles was to be the second runner to carry the torch on its way from Greece. She was an Australian of Greek descent. She was not only a gifted athlete but also very pretty. She was perfect. She was us, the new Australia.

Then suddenly the old Australia showed its face, rearing up from deep in the CBD.

Yianna Souleles was bumped.

In her place would be . . . Kevan Gosper's eleven-year-old daughter.

Sophie Gosper, said the *Sydney Morning Herald*, is too young by one year to run with the torch in Australia, but was invited by the Greeks to participate in their ten-day relay.

And how did that happen?

SOCOG chief executive Sandy Hollway said he did not know how the decision had come about but denied that the Gosper family had jumped the queue.

He described the issue as a storm in a teacup.

The same article also reported that Mr Gosper was already under investigation by the IOC ethics commission over allegedly accepting excessive hospitality during Salt Lake City's successful 2002 Winter Olympics bid.

The *Herald* said that Gosper denied having anything to do with the decision to make his daughter the first Australian torch-bearer in the Olympic relay.

And that was pretty much that.

Sydney was momentarily outraged but Gosper never felt the need to apologise, and whatever disturbance was caused has since been washed as smooth as the sand on Bondi Beach.

CHAPTER ELEVEN

TAKE THE CAR.

No.

Why not?

I don't want to.

You're getting a taxi all the way to Ledoux's place? That's like fifty bucks.

No, I'll get the ferry to Manly then take the bus.

It'll take you hours, Peter. Please take my car.

Kelvin was my friend. I should have been able to confess my problem with the bridge, but instead I lied.

It's for the book, I said. I want to write about the CBD, about the Manly Ferry.

CHAPTER TWELVE

THERE ARE FEW THINGS more pleasing, suggested
Governor Phillip, who never had the misfortune
to see what I saw later that morning when I
walked through the shadows of the Central Business District, all the way from Town Hall Station
down to Circular Quay where I intended to catch
the Manly Ferry. There are few things more
pleasing, reflected the senior-ranking white
man, sitting inside his very badly constructed
house, dipping his goose quill into his ink pot
to write: nothing is more pleasing than the con-
templation of order and useful arrangement,
arising gradually out of our tumult and confu-
sion; and perhaps this satisfaction cannot anywhere be more fully enjoyed than where a
settlement of civilised people is fixing itself upon
a newly discovered or savage coast.

He had proclaimed this wild place 'Sydney', although its inhabitants continued to call it 'the camp' for many years to come. The Tank Stream ran down its centre. Tents and huts were lined up north-south and east-west, drawn up in ranks facing the parade ground, with the convicts' tents in long neat rows close by. Introducing a class distinction that you can see in Sydney 210 years later, the convicts and marines were Westies, relegated to this area to the west of the Tank Stream, while the governor and his officers took possession of the east.

This plan of Sydney, recorded in a detailed map made thirty-five days after the first arrival of the whites, shows us a town in its moment of greatest possibility. It was, of course, a prison camp so a convict had already struck a marine with a cooper's adze and been sentenced to receive fifty lashes. Another had committed a petty theft and been marooned out on the island of Pinchgut to see how he liked a starvation diet of bread and water. But no one had yet had the flesh flayed from their spine. There had not yet been murder. The Eora tribe had not been decimated by smallpox. The convicts and the blacks had not quite begun that dreadful battle that continues to this day. The Tank Stream was not sullied by the pigs. The soldiers and their prisoners had not yet instigated those little crooked deals which would poison the moral groundwater for centuries to come. The officers were not yet trading in rum or using the free supply of slave labour to transform themselves into country gentlemen. At this moment, while 300 men huddled in tents with their crops already wilting in the sun, the commandant of this little gulag actually began to imagine an extraordinary city. Governor Arthur Phillip summoned up 'Sydney'; he willed it into being.

Lines are there traced out, he wrote, which distinguish the principal street of an intended town, to be terminated in the governor's house, the main guard and the criminal court. In some parts of this space temporary barracks at present stand, but no permanent buildings will be suffered to be placed except in conformity to the plan laid down. Should the town still be extended in future, the form of other streets is also traced in such a manner as to ensure the free circulation of air. The principal streets, according to this design, will be 200 feet wide.

It is the thought of those 200-foot-wide streets that takes your breath away today and when, fresh from my stroll on Bondi Beach, I walked through that unloved opportunistic CBD, as I entered the shadow of the monorail, that brutal artery grown to feed the multiplying mutant cells of Darling Harbour, I could only mourn the passing of this city of vistas, although God knows how long they ever were a possibility, for just a few months after Phillip described his town-plan the grand design seems to have given way to workaday expediency and there was a dirt track meandering from the governor's temporary quarters to the lieutenant governor's house and then pursuing a desultory course to the hospital buildings on the western side of the cove.

Phillip, who had begun by dreaming like Christopher Wren, now faced the daily question of putting up a shelter, any shelter, that would not collapse on its inhabitants. And now it became clear just how poorly provisioned this settlement was. Daniel Defoe had done a better job for Robinson Crusoe than the Home Office had done for Arthur Phillip. Soon the governor would write to Lord Sydney requesting better axes, better spades and better shovels, as those they had were the worst that ever were seen. In all his prisoners there were but fourteen carpenters. He had 300,000 nails but the trees were alien and seemed, to English eyes, unsuitable. The timbers were too hard, or twisted violently in the sun. The Aboriginals gave no clue, or none that an Englishman was prepared to follow, for the savages lived in caves around the harbour's edge or made temporary shelter by peeling bark from the strange rough-skinned trees.

There was no lime and so no mortar could be made. At first there seemed no clay suitable for bricks but even when clay was found and the settlers busied themselves extracting lime from the shell middens on the foreshores, there was not, in all that expensively provisioned fleet, a single man with any real experience of making bricks.

I was musing on this issue when I was interrupted by that opinionated fellow out of Flann O'Brien.

I believe you are wrong about the brick-making, said he. Is there not a museum in Sydney celebrating just such a chap?

You are thinking of James Bloodsworth?

I saw the very bricks he made. They have them stacked away like antique books.

Yes, but have you touched them? They crumble in your hand like tea cake. They are soft and sandy and fired at far too cool a temperature.

A 'master brick-maker and builder'. I quote exactly.

I don't believe Bloodsworth was a master. He was convicted of the theft of one game cock and two hens belonging to a baker from Surrey.

Note the baker. That is the heart of it. Agh, poor old Bloodsworth. He stole a loaf of bread, I do not doubt it.

Wait. I am attempting to show what human clay he was made of.

You are getting off the track, attacking poor Bloodsworth.

I am not off-track. I am showing you what material Governor Phillip had available to make his city with. At the time of Bloodsworth's trial there were two 'detainers' against the prisoner for burglary and he had also been charged on suspicion of being concerned in robberies and burglaries with 'the notorious gang that then infested the neighbourhood of Kingston'.

So the ruling class alleged.

Yes they did. Two of that gang were executed, another sentenced to transportation. But in Bloodsworth's case there was, I quote, a petition for mercy, signed by militiamen, day labourers and others of a very inferior situation, many others also of persons unknown in Kingston but not the name of a reputable tradesman belonging to the town except two who represented to me that they signed it to be relieved of incessant importunity.

And your point is?

On the strength of his associates, it is clear he

was not a master brick-maker, that he was probably as suited for making bricks as the timber of the cabbage-tree palm was suited for making houses.

Did he not build the first Government House?

Did not the building very nearly fall down around Governor Bligh's head?

Ah, they were hard times.

The times were hard, and making bricks was the worst job in the colony and carting the bricks was an extreme punishment. There were no horses or oxen and only three carts and the twelve convicts were in the harness pulling three-quarters of a ton.

They fired roof tiles as well but, no matter what the book says, no master brick-maker oversaw the process and the tiles were porous and when they became heavy with water the roofs collapsed, and so on, and so forth. The military lived in daub and wattle shanties. Two years after Phillip's first grand vision the houses and public buildings were springing up without regard for any plan at all.

And for a certain period of its history, the result seems to have been not uncharming. It is not parallelogramic and rectangular, said Trollope a century later. One may walk about it and lose the direction in which one is going. Streets running side by side occasionally converge – and they bend and go in and out, and wind themselves about, and are intricate.

Much of what 'Sydney' means was set in the difficult early years under Phillip, not merely its haphazard town-plan but also the character of its people. In these years you can look for the explanation of our persistent egalitarianism, our complicated relationship with authority, our belief that the government should care for us. The fact that soldiers and convicts starved together forged us in a kind of fire, and in this – no matter what cruel sign our city was born under – we were fortunate indeed.

But the actual nature of the modern Central Business District, its curiously unloved opportunistic aesthetic, owes more to forces that were not able to properly flex their muscles until Governor Arthur Phillip sailed for home.

Phillip left behind a colony in which convict labour was intended for the 'public good', an iron-fisted but paternalistic social economy that the historian M.H. Ellis quaintly describes as 'socialistic'.

In the following two-year period, while they waited for the next naval man to take the post of governor, the colony was administered by military men, Grose and Johnston. Grose, amiably

Peter Carey

declaring himself to have no talent for adminis-
tration, gave Captain John Macarthur the power
to do the job on his behalf. As a result, when
Governor Hunter finally arrived in September
1795 he discovered a very particularly Australian
form of capitalism at work.

Doubtless following Macarthur's advice,
Grose had rewarded his men with generous land
grants. Every officer, Hunter recorded with surprise, had nearly 100 acres under cultivation: I
mean, he wrote, with stock and all; the poorest of
which will return wheat or other grain into store
from one hundred and two hundred pounds
this year.

But the soldiers were not only turned farmer,
they were merchants too. Macarthur's wife described it blithely thus: The officers in the colony,
with a few others possessed of money or credit in
England, unite together and purchase the cargoes
of such vessels as repair to this country from
various quarters. Two or more are chosen from
the number to bargain for the cargo offered for
sale, which is then divided among them, in pro-
portion to the amount of their subscriptions.

What she does not say is that the cargoes were
almost always rum and that the military were like
drug-dealers, buying and selling liquor to rank-
and-file soldiers, emancipated convicts, convicts

with free time – in fact anyone who worked for wages would accept no other currency but rum. It was also agreed to be a far better enticement to labour than any number of lashes.

At first Hunter declared this curious form of private enterprise 'a very great success', but less than three years later, locked in conflict with the powerful Macarthur, he was finding it necessary to explain to London how such a thing as the Rum Corps could come into existence. The officers chartered the *Britannia*, he wrote to the colonial secretary, a large quantity of spirits were imported, and trade began with the settlers and the lower orders of the people, the effects of which will long be felt.

And this man, Hunter complained, this man [Macarthur] so strenuous an advocate of such order and good management was one of the most extensive dealers in the colony. To this unfortunate system, founded upon all the ruins of all decency and civil order, all our misfortunes and expenses have been owing.

John Macarthur was fierce and he was clever, and if he was not an easy character to like, then neither was Hunter. They were two pit bulls in the ring, and Macarthur won and Hunter was recalled. Then Governor King arrived. He was the representative of the king and parliament, but

Macarthur was like an early version of Rupert Murdoch or Kerry Packer. It was he who wielded power over those ostensibly in charge.

When Governor King did not suit Macarthur he had him sent back home.

Governor Bligh replaced King in 1806, fresh from his disgrace on the *Bounty*. We might imagine Bligh was weakened, but he did not feel so. Like Macarthur, he did not have a deal of time for powers which were too far away. He was the law in this colony just as he had been the law upon his ship.

What have I to do with sheep, sir? he demanded of Macarthur, who was attempting to establish what would become Australia's most important industry. What have I to do with your cattle? Are you to have such flocks of sheep and herds of cattle as no man ever heard of before? No, sir, I have heard of your concerns, sir.

Was Bligh wrong to be outraged by Macarthur, to find men become very rich with free land and convict labour while, at the same time, he observed: the public buildings ruined from want of repairs, granaries not water-tight, Government House nearly uninhabitable, the town houses miserably neglected and the fort and churches at Sydney and Parramatta only half built.

He describes the officers as so connected by property and intercourse with the emancipated convicts both men and women that their influence affected public justice. As for the rank and file, they were, he said, engrafted with the convicts to a man.

Further, the new governor found that people had been constructing houses where they were forbidden to build. They had been given leases but the leases were improper. They had, for instance, built on the domain which Governor Phillip had clearly indicated as a park. Although he acted with the typical bullying brutality which had brought about the mutiny on the *Bounty* and would produce a second mutiny in Sydney Cove, we can thank God he did do. He reclaimed that great park which we enjoy today. If he had not done so we can be confident that the Rum Corps would never have arranged a replacement.

Of course, in this great frenzy of knocking down, the king's representative made the mistake of coming up against Captain John Macarthur.

Macarthur had a lease on land to the east of the new St Philip's Church. I do not know if Bligh was correct in asserting that this land belonged not to the captain but to the church. Still, he hated Macarthur so that was not the point. Like others, Macarthur had a lease, but the lease meant nothing to Bligh who cautioned: Those people holding allotments without any buildings thereon I have warned that whatever they erect will be at their own risk . . .

Now there were many steps, including a court case too complicated to go into here, that led to the moment when Macarthur wrote that letter which would open him to the charge of treason, to the moment when Governor Bligh was dragged out from under the bed where he had so ignobly fled the rebels, but his not unreasonable insistence on town planning played some part in his downfall.

For in his attempt to tidy up the mess which Sydney had become, he had given his most powerful adversary joint cause with the common people who were already in a panic lest the land they thought theirs should be taken away from them.

In the story of the so-called Rum Rebellion it is always Bligh who is the bad guy, and while we would never want another Captain Bligh we might at least allow that there is no one else in our history who had the balls to stand up against the opportunism and cronyism of the Rum Corps or those spiritual descendants who the libel laws forbid us to name.

The modern CBD is their living monument, a

tribute to an élite which places very little value on the public good.

If there were not that opera house and that harbour just down the road you might accept that you were somewhere provincial and uninspired, but Sydney is not uninspired and on the edges of the CBD, on the rocks at Bennelong Point, you get some glimpse not only of what we were, but what we might yet become.

On this sunny April morning it was a great relief to escape the chill of the monorail, to walk briskly under the deep senseless shadows of the Cahill Expressway, and out on to the quay, down the number three wharf, and to board the Manly Ferry with just twenty seconds to spare.

Climbing to the top deck I find myself in a different world, one in which even the harbour bridge seems to me a thing of joy, its two hinges joining beneath a blinking red aviation light.

In a sea of dancing silver flashes the ferry pulls around that great pink platform on which the opera house stands. That any city would have this masterpiece is extraordinary, but in the city of the Rum Corps it is a miracle.

CHAPTER THIRTEEN

JACK LEDOUX HAD PROMISED that his friend Peter Myers would talk about Earth, and that was the only reason I came to Sydney University at six o'clock on a rainy autumn evening. I took a seat in a steep raked lecture theatre in the Faculty of Architecture. When Peter Myers appeared, I obediently opened my notebook and uncapped my pen. No student was ever more eager to hear about midden heaps and lime and convict clay.

Myers was a bearded grizzled man of average build with a friendly appearance and a dry understated humour. I wished he would speak a little more loudly and would not refer to presumably famous people by first names but he was, after all, an architect talking with other architects and no one had invited me to eavesdrop.

Eschewing projection or anything overly actorly, he began, in the manner of one resuming an old conversation, by recalling his visit to an exhibition of Alvar Aalto's work in London and finding it, well, very *ordinary*, and intuiting that there was something missing in this narrative of Alvar Aalto's success. So he said to his friend who had worked with Alvar Aalto, did Aalto have blue eyes?

And his friend said, oh yes, intensely blue. He was very charismatic.

QED, said Peter Myers, it was proven.

What was?

Why, Peter Myers' belief that you should trust your hunches, and what he was to talk about tonight (although this would be a big surprise to me) was how it was that the opera-house competition jury selected the work of a Dane, Joern Utzon.

Now the generally accepted explanation is that the American architect Eero Saarinen used his authority to PUSH this design through the reluctant jury. What is implicit here is the commonly shared assumption that we would never, not in a million years, have selected this building without a lot of outside help.

Graham Jahn's *Sydney Architecture* puts it like this: An extraordinary site on Sydney Harbour at

Peter Carey

Bennelong Point, an ambitious state premier (Joe Cahill), a visiting American architect (Eero Saarinen) and a young Dane's billowy sketches were the key factors which generated one of the most important modern buildings.

Vincent Smith, in *The Sydney Opera House*, tells the story thus: The winning design had been already marked down to go on the shortlist when Saarinen arrived (late) for the judging.

When, writes Smith, he saw Joern Utzon's drawings – having been on the site only hours before – he was wildly enthusiastic. It was an extraordinary and complex proposal and the other judges had their reservations. But to every objection they made Saarinen had an answer. He convinced them, though it's hard to believe that their objections to the design were terribly strong. They WERE looking at a monumental building.

It was already obvious that Peter Myers was not someone to burst into an argument directly through the front door. Whatever his thesis was, he was *sidling* into it, telling us that he had been a student in London in the late 1960s and had demonstrated outside that great brutal concrete fort, the American Embassy in Grosvenor Square, and that the designer of that building had been Eero Saarinen.

And here was his intuition – that the man who

designed this dreadful embassy could not, no matter what he claimed, *possibly* have been the champion of Utzon's opera house.

I was ready to follow him but Myers seemed to lose interest in that line of argument and now he returned to Alvar Aalto, alleging he had stolen the work of an architect. Plisjker? Fisketjon? My hearing had been ruined by the Stihl chainsaw and now I could not get the fellow's name no matter how I strained towards it. Just the same, Myers' point was clear: when Alvar Aalto built his plagiarised building he got great reviews, as if the critics didn't know that he had pinched it.

I was fearful Myers had lost his way, but I underestimated him for now he showed us that Aalto and Saarinen were men in parallel. Saarinen was the architect of that floating shell-like structure, the TWA terminal at JFK, which is always thought of as living proof of his sympathy with Utzon. But no. Trust your intuitions, said Peter Myers. The present TWA building was not Saarinen's original design. Before he flew to Sydney to sit on the opera-house jury Saarinen had a clumpish modernist design for the TWA terminal. After Sydney he redrew the plans.

In a moment Myers would name the English architect Leslie Martin as the man of power amongst the jury and he would chart a dazzling, almost Byzantine map delineating Leslie Martin's lines of artistic and political force, showing a man of taste and discernment well accustomed to quietly wielding influence. But first, casually, almost accidentally, he came to Earth. He reminded us of the site the Sydney Opera House would stand on.

At the time of the competition that sandstone point was occupied by an abandoned tram terminus, a crenulated fort of monumental ugliness, but in 1788 it had been the site of the first shell kiln. There were, said Peter Myers, middens, great piles of shells abandoned after meals, and these middens were twelve METRES HIGH on that site, evidence of ancient occupation. This was the first city of Sydney.

He reminded us that the city of the Rum Corps and the convicts was therefore the *second* historic city of Sydney and explained how the second city died when the Cahill Expressway cut across the quay. The city was blindfolded, he said, only waiting to be executed.

With the city physically isolated from the harbour, only Bennelong Point was left, free, unfettered. The Sydney Opera House competition was the big chance for Sydney to escape the creeping mediocrity it had become.

And it was then I saw what Myers was up to.

He was actually addressing the great question of Sydney. By what divine intercession were we granted that opera house? Why us? How come?

The first champion of the Sydney Opera House was clearly Eugene Goossens, the conductor of the Sydney Symphony Orchestra, and it was he, as early as 1948, who identified this as a perfect site for a performing-arts centre. For years he talked, politicked, addressed the issue in public and in private, and in 1956, with the site chosen and the competition already underway, he was arrested by HM Customs with pornography in his luggage. In what was a spooky funhouse mirror image of Utzon's final departure, Goossens was hounded out of Sydney and Australia. Like Utzon, he never returned.

Myers now turned his attention to the jurors, sifting through them, looking for our benefactor.

There was Colin Parkes, the New South Wales state architect, the son of Sir Henry Parkes, the so-called 'father of federation'. Without doubt he was not Utzon's first champion.

The professor of architecture at Sydney University was the second jury member. Professor Ashworth had served with distinction in the Second World War, and was a lieutenant colonel at its end. It was he, Peter Myers explained, who selected Leslie Martin.

Myers then projected a transparency which showed two books, one by Leslie Martin, one by Professor Ashworth, each bearing the same title: *Flats*.

Meaning? That their characters and value were here clearly contrasted. On the left, the dull but useful Ashworth. On the right, the elegant designer, the connoisseur Leslie Martin.

Peter Myers then projected an image of a third book, *Circle*. The authors: Leslie Martin and Naum Gabo.

What was this about? Why, open the book and you can find work by Arup, the engineer who would finally work on Utzon's opera house. Thus proving? Thus proving that Arup knew Martin, that it was Martin who brought in Arup at the end, that Martin was the quiet puppet master of the show.

Utzon, according to Peter Myers, always understood that Leslie Martin was the most important judge. Utzon would have read Leslie Martin's book. He would have been aware of Leslie Martin's design for the Royal Festival Hall in London. And now Myers alerted us to the strong similarities between these two large performance spaces, both addressing water, both sitting on a kind of platform.

He reminded us that the brief for the Sydney

Opera House required two halls, one seating 3,500 and the other 1,200. He showed an image of the Royal Festival Hall and then, presto, he was a magician. He doubled the image, so there were two identical halls side by side, and what did you have?

The Sydney Opera House on the River Thames? Not quite, but imagine a man of genius beginning this way, just as Picasso might take Velázquez perhaps, and by a series of daring steps arrive at something new. The double image of the festival hall looked like two captives, blocks of stone from which the masterwork would soon be carved.

This is how culture works, asserted Myers. The Sydney Opera House is Joern Utzon recasting the Royal Festival Hall in such a way that Martin will understand. So the opera house is an esoteric letter from the architect to the most powerful member of the jury.

There is not the slightest doubt, said Peter Myers, that Martin would immediately decode this compliment, this fabulously sophisticated, dazzlingly successful attempt to take his own work and turn it into something even more wonderful. Amongst the proofs that he continued to pull out of his sleeve was Utzon's perspective drawing of the opera house.

The Conditions of Competition (item no. 7) required *perspective drawing of such elevation as the competitor may select as his main elevation and/or approach to the building*. Utzon chose, instead, to insist on what he had done, to emphasise the doubling, and he audaciously rendered, not the two halls in perspective, but the space *between* them.

He heightened the drawing with gold leaf, said Peter Myers, which is perhaps one reason none of the drawings were shown to the public. This one with the gold leaf might be deemed to have broken the rules of the competition.

Finally it was Saarinen who rendered the required perspective drawing of Utzon's opera house, and to that extent he was the hero for without this drawing the design could not have won.

Well he had convinced me, but Peter Myers would not leave well enough alone, and now he was driven to prove that both Utzon's and Martin's designs related to a famous building in Copenhagen and that each of their designs were, in a sense, a conversation, a love letter written to another building, invisible to all but them.

Enough.

At past seven, just as he produced issue number two of the *Architects' Yearbook* (of which Leslie

Martin was the editor), I had to stand, not just because I was out of my depth, but because I was late for David Williamson's play *The Great Man* which had recently begun its Sydney season in the Drama Theatre of the opera house, a space which was not even indicated in the original brief and which was one of those indications that Utzon would inherit a client who not only gives bad information about the nature of the site but also changes his mind continually.

I slink out of the lecture theatre, out into the dark rainy streets of City Road where – another miracle – I find a taxi.

CHAPTER FOURTEEN

I WAS MUCH SURPRISED at the fortifications of Sydney Harbour, wrote Anthony Trollope. Fortifications, unless specially inspected, escape even a vigilant seer of sights, but I, luckily for myself, was enabled specially to inspect them. I had previously no idea that the people of New South Wales were either so suspicious of enemies, or so pugnacious in their nature. I found five separate fortresses, armed, or to be armed, to the teeth with numerous guns, – four, five, six at each point; – Armstrong guns, rifled guns, guns of eighteen tons of weight, with loopholed walls, and pits for riflemen as though Sydney were to become another Sebastopol. I was shown how the whole harbour and city were commanded by these guns. There were open batteries and casemented batteries, shell rooms and powder magazines, barracks rising here and trenches dug there. There was a boom to be placed across the harbour and a whole world of torpedoes ready to be sunk beneath the water, all of which were prepared and ready to use in an hour or two. It was explained to me that 'they' could not possibly get across the trenches, or break the boom, or escape the torpedoes, or live for an hour beneath the blaze of guns . . . But in viewing these fortifications, I was most especially struck by the loveliness of the sites chosen. One would almost wish to be a gunner for the sake of being at one of these forts.

Trollope was in my mind as the departing Manly Ferry scraped, iron on wood, along the wharf at Circular Quay that Monday morning.

If only you would get your head out of books, said a by now familiar voice. Look around you. Is it not a lovely sight?

Yes, I answered, but the book helps you see this landscape better. It is the book that shows you that this city has been shaped by its defences. Over there, to the left, where the bridge sticks its claws in the rock, was once Fort Dawes. And there on Bennelong Point, where the opera house is, that was Fort Macquarie, the ugliest thing Greenway ever designed. And a few hundred metres north is Pinchgut . . .

Don't mention Francis Morgan . . .

. . . who was hung in chains until he fell apart. Pinchgut's proper name is Fort Denison.

Behind Fort Denison is the naval dockyard of Garden Island where you can see that great ugly cream-brick structure, so typical of Australian barracks architecture. This five acres of inner-city waterfront is still controlled by the Defence Department.

On the north shore, directly north of Farm Cove, five acres of splendid gardens tumble down towards the sandstone cliffs and there, behind that armed policeman, is the sandstone mansion of Admiralty House. It was, for many years, the home of the British admiral commanding the British squadron in Australia.

Time and again the armed forces have taken possession of the most beautiful land on Sydney Harbour. Five bays along from Kirribilli House you will find that great scabby finger of Bradleys Head. In 1880 Sydney waited to engage the Russian navy here. We had a proper fortress, mighty cannons, pyramids of balls encased by nets. There are photographs, taken very soon after Trollope's visit. They show three white-helmeted gunners posing at the fortress with folded arms. Behind them – the yellow sandstone cliffs of Sydney Heads.

After Bradleys Head the Manly Ferry passes Chowder Bay and the wild wooded headland of Georges Head. According to the splendid map reproduced on page twenty-five of *Reflection on a Maritime City – An Appreciation of the Trust Lands on Sydney Harbour*, an enemy craft following the ferry's present course, north-north-east in twelve fathoms, is passing into a deadly barrage of fire. On the north-west shore, in that forested hillside where those white cockatoos rise in a raucous crowd, those same shell rooms and powder magazines and barracks can still be found, pretty much as Trollope saw them. Together with one hundred and fifteen acres of waterfront bush, they are in the process of being returned to the public.

The map was made in 1880 and revised again in 1917. It shows Trollope's battery as the locus of a radius which swings in a defensive arc across the harbour, a fine grey line intersected by other thicker arcs representing first artillery, then searchlights, and other signs I cannot understand. I can count eleven of these arcs all crowding around the Heads, one with its locus at Georges Head, others at North Head and South Head, one centred at that very place on New South Head Road where Jack Ledoux and I stopped to admire the yellow cliffs above the empty Pacific

Ocean. At that time I had grappled for an explanation of those tiny windows in that ugly block of flats – why anyone would place this life-denying style in such a spectacular setting. But when I saw the map of these shore batteries, the style at last made sense.

If Sydney was a fort then would not the barracks be a part of our architectural vernacular? Did not those awful flats on Old South Head Road bear a close resemblance to barracks buildings at Chowder Bay, Garden Island Naval Dockyard and Cockatoo Island as well? You do not join the army to admire the view.

Now, said my persistent companion, you are mocking Sydney.

No, I am explaining some awful architecture.

Yes, but in the end you are claiming the citizens are nervous nellies. 'The Russians are invading!' 'Napoleon is coming!' You make them appear ridiculous. What interest would Napoleon have in it, for Jesus' sake? This was well before the surfing craze.

They were not mistaken at all. As a young man Napoleon sought to ship with La Perouse. If he had had his wish he would have been in Botany Bay at the same time as the First Fleet. We know Napoleon never lost his interest in Sydney.

I suppose the city was teeming with his spies.

You need not smirk. There is evidence of one at least. François Pèron. A famous naturalist. He reported the fortifications of Sydney in great detail. It was invasion that was on his mind.

And you will not refrain from quoting, I suppose?

I will not, no. To the right at the north point of Sydney Cove, you perceive the signal battery, which is built upon a rock difficult of access: six pieces of cannon, protected by a turf entrenchment, cross their fire with that of another battery which I shall presently mention.

He does sound like a spy, I warrant.

Pèron concluded Sydney Harbour was too well fortified a place to attack. But he thought they could invade at Broken Bay.

Correct me if I am wrong, but the only attack in Sydney Harbour was the Japanese in 1942, and that is long ago and best forgotten in the present climate.

That alters nothing. This harbour is a fort. It is this which makes its bones. You can see this in a satellite photograph. Immense fortifications all showing bright red from the Heads to Sydney Cove.

It is only the trees that show bright red.

Yes, and for 200 years those we trusted with our city's defence have also defended eighty acres at Bradleys Head from developers and their mates in government. They likewise saved 115 acres at Georges Head in Chowder Bay. There are 183 more acres at North Head, another thirty-odd acres at South Head. They still control that multi-layered midden heap of a site at Cockatoo Island. They have not only saved us priceless green space but a great deal of delicate history as well. I offer as my first exhibit the road to Bungaree's farm.

I know that name. He was the most famous Aboriginal ever born. Did not he go to London and meet the king?

That was Bennelong. This was Bungaree who travelled with Matthew Flinders on his great voyages of exploration. Also he was a great favourite of Governor Macquarie who seems to have had the impertinent idea that he would civilise him. Macquarie got a passion to settle Bungaree and his relatives on a European-style farm.

There's a folly for you.

Indeed it was. On Tuesday January 31, 1815, which was the governor's birthday, Macquarie and his wife and a large party of ladies and gentlemen were rowed the six miles down the harbour to Georges Head, the same place where the battery and arsenal and barracks were later constructed.

Here the governor decorated Bungaree with a brass gorget, declaring him 'Chief of the Broken Bay Tribe', and he showed Bungaree his farm on which he had constructed huts for his people.

Bungaree must have thought this a mighty joke.

Bungaree's people starting working with great zeal, but soon they sold off their tools and returned to their earlier way of life.

You began telling this because you claimed some delicate history had been saved by these military occupations?

Yes, Macquarie made a road from the beach up to the farm.

Now you're going to say the road is still there?

I think it is. I walked across the abandoned submarine base at Chowder Bay, up across the bitumen, into the bush where I was shown a steep overgrown path about six feet wide.

What a foolish sentimental monument. What a thing to be preserved.

Geoff Bailey, who is the head of the interim planning committee for these old defence sites, would not make an absolute claim but there is no other good explanation for the road's existence. It starts out from the best place for the ladies and gentlemen to come ashore, it is the right width for a cart, it leads to the place where the farm seems to have been. The farm itself was bulldozed years ago and turned into a playing field.

You were foolish to be so complimentary about the military.

Yes, but if you ever should be permitted to visit Cockatoo Island you'll see how the defence forces leave us a thousand times more history than real-estate developers.

What is it like? Take your time now.

A great plateau of sandstone which has been eroded and extended with successive landfills. Forsaken nineteenth-century prisons and barracks still occupy its crown. Down on the southern waterfront a desolate direct-current power station, its walls lined with mercury vapour flasks, sits waiting for its Frankenstein or Spielberg. A great tunnel cuts through its centre, from north to south, the most direct way for workers to pass from one side to the other. Two huge dry docks, where apprentices dived and swam in the boiling Sydney summers, lie abandoned. Cockatoo Island occupies less than one square mile, but it is difficult to imagine a more complex or satisfying historical site. Here you'll find convict barracks adapted as Second World War air-raid shelters, with nineteenth-century sandstone walls topped by brutal concrete three foot thick.

No respect for history here.

Yes, the disrespect is perfect. Let me give you another example. The first convicts were put to work, cutting huge narrow-necked grain silos into the living rock of the plateau.

Years later a new machine shop was needed so a great slice of the mother rock, from plateau to sea level, was carved away. That this destroyed six of the convict silos was, naturally enough, no obstacle, but that great brutal slice through the rock now shows the silo better than any curator might have dreamed. If the visitor pushes his back hard against the corrugated-iron wall of the abandoned machine shop, if he shades his eye against the sun, he can see in transverse section a twelve-foot-high carafe carved from the top of the plateau.

Now, of course, we must decide what will be done with these sites the defence forces have kept for us.

Shut up.

I'll not shut up. Did I say parts of the island are very beautiful, tree-lined walks with cottages and views the equal of nothing in the world?

Shut up, stop talking to yourself. That fellow with the beard is staring at you.

My God, it's Sheridan, my friend.

Not another word to me.

As the shambolic man with the greying beard came walking towards me, grinning lopsidedly, the ferry arrived at Manly Wharf with such force that he staggered sideways.

Perfect, he cried as we embraced, completely fucking perfect.

CHAPTER FIFTEEN

NOW HERE IS THE thing, said Sheridan as we came down off the wharf in Manly which had been a very pretty village in 1888 but these days has the very democratic odour of tomato sauce about it. Here's the thing, he said, slinging the coil of yellow rope over his broad shoulder as we pushed through the crowd around the sushi bar. I am not actually going home right now. I've come to pick up the Merc and then I'm going up to the Blue Mountains.

Are you climbing?

No, he said, I'm not. Why are you coming to see me this bloody way?

I shrugged. I could not tell him I was not going to see him. I was off to collect that story from Jack Ledoux.

Were you trying to avoid the bridge?

When did I tell you about the bridge?

I always think of Kurt Vonnegut when you call me. How does it go? I'm an old fart now and my breath smells of mustard gas and roses and I like to get drunk and call my old friends in the middle of the night. Last time you called you said you were going to come to the mountains with me, or did you forget that too?

Well I'm writing a book about Sydney.

The Blue Mountains are part of Sydney.

Sherry, it's eighty miles to Katoomba.

Jesus, Peter, the mountains are the jail walls of Sydney. They are connected, physically, geologically, dramatically. You cannot write about Sydney and leave out the Blue Mountains. He put his big arm around my shoulders. In this embrace I detected the musty smell of someone who had been sleeping on sofas, and I remembered what I had heard that morning on Bondi Beach, that Sherry had not only lost his wife but his job. He had written for the soaps for twenty years, but the producers were younger now and they would not tolerate his tirades against them.

You should have called when you arrived, he said. I went out to the airport but I had my information wrong.

I'll come, I said suddenly.

Of course you'll bloody come. He crushed me

violently against him and I felt all his need and frailty in his mighty chest.

But first, he said, you're going to meet this amazing man. You cannot write a book about Sydney and leave him out. And then he was off, walking as fast as he was talking, head down, arms flailing, enthusing about the mechanic who kept his 33-year-old 230S running. In 400 yards of pavement he covered a whole life story – the guy had a PhD in philosophy and lost his wife and became an alcoholic and survived for five years collecting empty cans and bottles and then became a car thief until he fell in love with this blonde surfie chick with a rusted-out Merc and now he fixed Mercs.

When I first knew Sheridan he lived with winos and derros on the street in Darlinghurst and he later published a wonderful book of photographs and life stories. When drunk he was inclined to talk of this book bitterly, as the high point of his moral life.

As it turned out the mechanic was not there. The roller door was down and locked, and Sheridan's car was parked out in the lane with the key hidden somewhere in the tangle of the back seat. If the paintwork was chalkier than the last time I saw it, the interior had not changed – Coke cans and cigarette packs on the floor, the back seat filled with ropes, climbing boots, camping equipment and a great assortment of books and papers.

You'll meet him later, said Sheridan as we ground slowly up the hill out of Manly. He grinned at me and showed the big white teeth in the middle of his hairy face.

Fuck it. We'll go along the Parramatta Road.

It's the long way round.

Who gives a fuck? You can't write about Sydney and leave out the Parramatta Road.

This was my first warning that Sheridan's sometimes worrying enthusiasm was being put at the service of my project. He had not only made room for me inside the car, he was now altering his plans to suit what he understood to be the nature of my enquiry.

Parramatta Road is like the city's spine, he said, it was the most important road in the colony. When they couldn't get anything to grow in Sydney Cove they found better ground in Parramatta.

Rose Hill, it was called.

That's right, said Sheridan, raising his eyebrows in delight. Exactly. Rose fucking Hill.

So we drove back into the city, across the bridge, which caused me not the least anxiety when someone else was driving, and in half an hour, having made a stop for the Diet Coke which Sheridan was now drinking in terrifying quantity, we tooled along the charmless de-natured landscape which is the Parramatta Road.

This is Sydney, declared Sheridan, throwing his empty Coke can into the back seat. The harbour is peripheral. The harbour is not a place that anyone can afford to live. Parramatta is the geographic centre of Sydney.

This is not an attractive drive, Sherry.

Did I say it was? The thing is, Pete, it's historic.

Historic? All I could see were car yards and flapping plastic flags and garish sanserif signs CRAZY BARRY'S DISCOUNT PRICES. It was a smaller uglier version of Route 17 in New Jersey.

Look, screamed Sheridan, I can tell you're not looking.

Well there's an old bullnose verandah, I said.

No, fuck the verandah, said Sheridan, ponderously overtaking a marginally slower truck. Just ask yourself why the most important road in the colony would be filled with car yards. Come on, this is your family history, Pete. Didn't your grandfather have a stables? Weren't your family horse traders? Yes? Didn't your granddad go on to taxis and T-model Fords? Well, this is how it was with the Parramatta

Road. This is where the stables were, where the
horse traders were.

How do you know that?

It's obvious. This was the only fucking road. It
led to John Macarthur. All the governors rode
this way when they came out to pay their respects
to old Captain Rum Corps. When Bligh wanted
to inform John Macarthur he was prohibited
from building on his allotment, he sent the poor
old surveyor general galloping along this road.
These car yards are historic markers. I'd put a
fucking brass plaque on every one.

Did we actually have to come here so you
could tell me that?

Yes, said Sheridan, as we finally turned from
the desolation of Parramatta Road on to the
freeway, you gotta understand what is hidden.

Ahead of us we could see the Blue Mountains,
very low and exceedingly blue with all those
millions of drops of eucalyptus oil refracting
the sunlight.

Don't look like nothing, do they? It's like the
Parramatta Road. You can look at it and never
know.

I never liked the drive up here, I said.

Fuck the drive. I'm trying to educate you. You
know nothing about these mountains, mate, no
offence, except maybe sitting in the Fork 'n' View

and getting pissed on a Sunday lunch, so I am attempting, because I like you in spite of the fact that you have come home twice and not called me – I'm over that – but I'm trying to point out how deceptive the mountains are. In fact, I have just been reading Darwin, and he came here, yes, the great bloody Charles Darwin, and you can see the patronising shitbag getting it so wrong – that is until he finally understands what he is messing with. It's there on the back seat. Get it. Read it to me, in that cardboard box with all the paper.

I twisted myself into the back seat and finally discovered, beneath a tangle of plastic bags, a book.

Sheridan, this looks valuable. It's really old.

It's a book. There are Post-its. Read it, Pete, for Christsake.

I obeyed, reading the words Sheridan had underlined in brutal ballpoint pen: From their absolute altitude, Darwin had written, I expected to have seen a bold chain of mountains crossing the country; but instead of this, a sloping plain presents merely an inconsiderable front to the low land near the coast.

Stop, said Sheridan, now skip ahead to where I marked it down there. If you're not going to finish that Coke you can give it to me. There, at the top of the page, that's where Darwin finally realises what he's messing with. Following down a little valley . . . read it.

Following down a little valley and its tiny rill of water, I read, an immense gulf unexpectedly opens through the trees which border the pathway, at a depth of perhaps 1,500 feet. Walking on a few yards, I read, one stands at the brink of a vast precipice, and below one sees a grand bay or gulf, for I know not what other name to give it, thickly covered with forest. The point of view is situated as if at the head of a bay, the line of cliff diverging on each side, and showing headland behind headland, as on a bold sea coast.

Fast forward. I've marked it lower.

Very early in the morning?

Good fellow.

Very early in the morning I walked about three miles to Govett's Leap: a view of similar character with that near the Weatherboard, but perhaps even more stupendous. So early in the day the gulf was filled with a thin blue haze, which although destroying the general effect of the view added to the apparent depth at which the forest was stretched out beneath our feet. These valleys which so long presented an insuperable barrier to the attempts of the most enterprising of the colonists . . .

That's the other thing, cried Sheridan, tearing

the book violently from my hand and returning it whence it came, these mountains are a massive fact of life. Darwin could travel here along the road, but for thirty years these mountains had been impassable. The convicts and their jailers were locked up together, chained together on the coast. There were eight fucking expeditions. Eight. They bashed their way up rivers and waterfalls. They had no idea how to live off the land so they carried all this shit with them. Tons of stuff, and they would just give up and turn back. Look at those mountains. They don't look like anything. Nothing is revealed, to quote the song. But they're older than the fucking Himalayas, and they are very fucking deep, mate.

So lunatics like you throw themselves over the edge on ropes.

Sheridan gave me a thoughtful look. Mmmm, he said, and, for the first time in our journey, fell silent.

There are a couple of things I could tell you, he began again, but I wouldn't want certain people to know I was, like, Deep Throat.

I'll change your name?

To what?

How about 'Sheridan'?

You sarcastic bugger, you never did believe I was descended from Sheridan.

Peter Carey

I do.

Then call me Sheridan, I don't give a fuck. Now we're coming up on to the mountains. This bit is steep but it gives no idea of the obstacles they had to overcome.

I remember the road now, and I began to recall why I had come here so rarely. It was not that I ever failed to be thrilled and astonished by the extraordinary drama of the Blue Mountains: the sublime vistas, the plunging waterfalls, the teetering stairs, the dizzy ledges, but this road always made me despondent. There was something so melancholy about the rusting electric railway lines running beside the little towns, something so stunted and mediocre in the architecture that I always became depressed on the way there and depressed on the way back.

You don't know what you're looking at, said Sheridan when I had confessed my feelings. You're lucky I'm with you.

I'm looking at ugly houses and a dreary railway line.

Yes, he said, and we came around a corner and he pulled the Merc languidly off the road. A coal truck blasted its horn and buffeted us.

Bring that tape recorder, said Sheridan and climbed out. I followed him a few yards, the tape

148

recorder in my hand. He escorted me to a tall gum.

Everything is hidden, said Sheridan, a mite pompously in my opinion. He gazed up into the umbrella of the tree.

Oh give us a break, I said, I've lived in the bush, Sheridan. This isn't the first gum tree I ever saw. I can recognise a koala's arse as well as anyone.

Where's the koala?

In answer two small droppings fell from the tree, bouncing on the lower branches and landing in the litter of the bush floor.

Sheridan raised his eyebrows at me. I suppose you know what I'm going to say next?

That the koala has even reduced the size of its brain to save on energy?

Will you turn on your tape recorder?

Why?

I heard that's what you were doing with Jack Ledoux.

I was shocked to see his eyes were blazing. He waited, his arms folded across his chest, until I had turned on the tape.

Now you can't write the name of the town, he began, but in one of these towns along here there is a pub where all the young fellows hang out. I like this pub, Pete, but it can be a pretty rough sort of a place and one night there is a brawl and

Peter Carey

this big raw-boned bastard, let's call him
Lurch . . .

Sheridan . . .

This fellow Lurch, said Sheridan firmly,
knocks the shit out of one of the young fellows.
Now Lurch is not only handy with his fists,
he is a great mate of the local cops, so he feels
pretty safe, but in his great excitement he
forgets that the poor fuck whose jaw he is busy
breaking just happens to be the son of the shire
president.

So when the kid has to be hospitalised his old
man doesn't take it lightly. He lays charges
against Lurch and then he fucking sues him,
and Lurch is down the gurgler to the sum of
sixty fucking thousand dollars.

Sheridan, why don't we do this later?

No, listen, said Sheridan, taking the tape recorder from my hand and speaking so directly
into it that the tape still reproduces the sound of
his saliva and the slight whistle of his breath.
Lurch then goes on to have a very successful
earth-moving business. Soon he has ten trucks
and front-end loaders and bulldozers and a couple of Bobcats. So the sixty thousand dollars has
not crippled him, but he cannot forgive the kid.
He hates this kid. Hates him, said Sheridan. And
his friend the cop hates him too, see? They don't

150

let him forget it either. They tell him, one day we'll get you, you bastard.

This is nuts. Let's sit in the car.

No. Now it's four years later and the kid who we will call . . . Paul, Paul and his mate go driving in his old man's perfectly restored '57 Chevrolet. This is a very precious piece of car and the boys are by now twenty-two, twenty-three years old and to cut a long story short they get piss-faced drunk and at four in the morning, with Paul at the wheel, the Chev leaves the road at speed . . .

Sheridan takes my arm and leads me around the tree to show me an ugly scar.

Right here, see, Pete. See.

We stand side by side staring at the tree.

They died?

Should have. This happens two hours before dawn. The road is deserted. It is freezing cold and foggy. But it is worse than that because Paul's mate has broken both his wrists.

Paul is piss-faced drunk but he knows he has given Lurch and the cop what they are waiting for. He has to get his mate to a hospital and when he does that the accident will be reported to the cops. *One day we'll get you, you bastard.* He knows he is going to go to jail.

His friend's name is Skink. He's a fabulous banjo player, but there is not a lot of him, hence the name. He's a skinny little lizard of a fellow and now the poor little bugger is lying on the frosty ground and both his wrists are shattered and he is in agony.

Don't worry, mate, says Paul, I'll walk into town and get an ambulance.

No you bloody won't, mate, says Skink.

Yes I bloody will.

No you bloody won't because if you do they'll put you in the bloody slammer and throw away the key.

Yes, I'm fucked.

Skink is one of them little freckle-faced fellows with sticky-out ears. You wouldn't expect big things of him, but now he tells Paul what he is going to do.

You're going to walk up the bloody road here, he says, and he directs him to that farm up there, you see that red old shed, just past there. That's my uncle's farm, says the kid. You wake him up and tell him you are taking his Fiat tractor and then you bring it back here.

I never drove a tractor.

You ain't got no fucking choice, mate, you're going to tow this bloody car away and I will tell you where you can put it where that fucking cop won't ever find it.

And this little skimpy kid lies there, on this very

spot, Pete, in the dark, in the fog. Can you imagine the pain? He lay on this spot while his friend came back with the tractor and then he waited while he towed the car away and hid it and then he waited for him to come back and drive him to hospital. Five hours that took.

That's a friendship, Pete. Do you have friends like that in New York City? I hope you do, mate. His fierce dark eyes were glistening. I have friends like that, he said, and then looked sharply away, as if embarrassed.

In the car again, he gave me back my tape recorder. See, I know what you're going to do with this fucking book. You're going to tell everyone how bent we are. I know this shit of yours. Convict colony, Rum Corps, etc., etc. Well, put in that story about those boys. That's Sydney for you, Peter. It's mates.

What will I say about the cop?

Oh don't you dare, cried Sheridan. Don't you dare make this a story about bent cops. You know I cannot bear it when you pull that shit.

CHAPTER SIXTEEN

THE SUBJECT OF THE New South Wales police force is a long and complicated one, more suited to Royal Commissions than a narrative like this. But the issue of corruption in Sydney is so pervasive that you cannot put your spade into the earth without coming up against it.

Here, a random witness – my friend, Geordie Levinson.

In 1974, said Geordie, who is exactly five foot four, I moved to Paddington with my girlfriend Sasha McPhee – a very tall girl. Sasha was mad about motor-cycles and she had a $700 trail bike which one morning was . . . simply *not* outside the house.

Of course it had been stolen and that was, to say the least, a nuisance. It was not insured and neither of us had much money. We'd just arrived from Melbourne and lots of things were wrong already. We didn't like where we were living. We were sharing the house. And now . . . $700 down the drain.

Sasha emptied her bank account and bought a second bike, and this time she insured it. Not long afterwards, ie a week, this second machine vanishes too.

The ink is not dry on the insurance claim when there is a knock on the door and this fellow introduces himself. Do you want his name? I'll make one up for you – Barry Williams.

So he says, hello, I'm Barry Williams.

I ask him what he wants.

You've lost a bike.

Yes, I said. We have. In fact we've lost two of them.

He seemed very pleasant, charming. He was well dressed too – Gucci loafers, chinos, polo shirt. Well, he said, if you come with me you can have your bike back.

So Sasha went with him and before too long the pair of them have returned and Sasha has the missing bike. Wires have been cut and are hanging off, but otherwise it's all in one piece.

So Sasha makes tea and the three of us sit at the kitchen table and she says to him, thank you very much.

Naturally I'm very curious about this transaction so, when neither of them explain it, I ask.

Well, says Sasha, Barry took me to a car park just up the road and the basement level is just *full* of bikes.

That's correct, says Barry. It's chocka.

And, says Sasha, Barry said here's your bike from the other night. You can have it back.

I did, says Barry. That's exactly what I said.

And I said, said Sasha, why are you giving it back?

And I said, Barry smiles, it seemed bad luck to lose two.

And I said, says Sasha, so you took the other one? And he said yes and so I ask him, why are you giving this one back?

Because, says Barry Williams, who was now sipping tea at my kitchen table, there's a *glut* on the market. More than we can sell. Also, she lost *two*.

I turned to Sasha but she only shrugged. Later I discovered that her only annoyance was that she had gotten back the one that was insured.

But I was upset, said Geordie, and I said to Barry Williams, what makes you think I wouldn't report this to the police?

He seemed astonished I would ask such a question. Why would you do that? You've got your bike back. Here we are, having a cup of tea. Anyway, it wouldn't do you any good.

But this is outrageous.

Well go to the cops if you like, mate. I'm just telling you, it won't do you any good.

Anyway, he was very calm. He took his time to finish his tea and when he left he shook my hand and wished me good luck. Meaning, I assumed, good luck with the police.

The instant he was gone I phoned Paddington police. They said they were the uniformed police, I better talk to the detectives, and so they gave me another number.

It took a long time for the detectives' phone to be picked up but finally a man answered. He didn't seem very interested. He said that someone would get back to me.

When? Tonight? Tomorrow?

Oh no, someone will get back to you.

But I was the only one who ever did any getting back. Not that it did me any good. Whenever I got hold of a detective, it always turned out to be the wrong person.

I forgot about it after a while and it would have been six months later that I called them again. But still I couldn't get them to pay attention.

Anyway, sometime later I'm walking down the street in Paddington and I run into Barry

Williams and I say, hi, what are you doing around here?

And he says, oh we're dismantling this fence. And it was a bluestone *wall*. And it looked terrific, it was a beautiful wall.

Are you taking it away?

Yes.

What for?

A commission.

A commission?

Yes, the owners are on holiday and we're taking the wall on commission for some people who want it.

Sometime later, said Geordie, there's a drinks party in the Eastern Suburbs. Beautiful house. Chandeliers. The people's name is Williams, and I say to my friend Victoria, these couldn't be any relation to Barry Williams?

That's the family. This is his parents' house.

No sooner has she said it, said Geordie, than I see Barry himself coming through the crowd.

That Barry Williams? But he's a crook in Paddington.

Yes, she said. He went to school at Cranbrook. He was there with so and so and so and so. And she reels off all these names of very wealthy people.

So why is he a thief?

Shush.

Barry catches sight of us, said Geordie, and he comes over, kisses Victoria on the cheek, shakes my hand as if we're old friends now. And in a strange way we are. That's Sydney, we're all so very intimately connected.

CHAPTER SEVENTEEN

IF YOU MAKE THIS book about yuppies like Geordie Levinson, said Sheridan, how can you expect to be taken seriously – he's not even from Sydney.

He's lived here twenty-five years.

Oh come on, Peter. He drives a Ferrari.

It was a Dino. Do you know how long ago that was?

Don't talk like a car dealer, said Sheridan who was now steering his great Queen Mother of a Merc down into the Megalong Valley. I don't give a fuck what he drives.

He was my lawyer. He still is my lawyer. You get to know a person very well that way. He is one of the most decent, fair-minded men I ever met.

He's a snob.

Sheridan, you've never spoken more than twenty words to him. Did he offend you in some way?

To be honest, Pete . . . he's five foot four.

Jesus, Sheridan.

As we left the heights of the mountain escarpment and descended through the coachwood forest, the chopped sunlight fell in bright slices across the chalky hood of the Merc. We had fleeting glimpses of the sandstone walls of the Blue Mountains rising above us, but we were no longer 'in the mountains'. As we came into the wider flatter land of the valley we left the bitumen and entered a dirt road and then a number of successively rougher dirt tracks until, after one particularly rocky passage, we stopped in front of a high and excessively complicated gate which bore all the marks of Sheridan's ingenious mind.

Once we were through this obstacle I asked him if we were now on his property but he was preoccupied with preserving the Merc's muffler. He swung on and off the track, unsuccessfully trying to avoid the rocks. When, after one violent thud, he cursed and stopped, it did not occur to me that we had arrived.

You should get a four-wheel drive, I said.

Sheridan turned those dark hurt eyes upon me.

The thing is, Pete, how does Geordie pull those chicks? What is he? Fifty? Fifty-five?

There was no point in telling him that Geordie now drove a Volvo station wagon, or that he was the father of three little boys. Geordie's current happiness would not have comforted my friend today.

Sheridan, I asked, are you OK?

He turned off the engine and, in the silence, bestowed upon me a sweet strained smile. Home sweet home, he said.

But there was no sign of any home and what sweetness there was in the over-grazed paddock was not immediately obvious.

Stuff to carry, he said.

I was soon loaded up with wine bottles and books and a very bloody leg of lamb around which the flies immediately clustered.

Where's the cave?

It's here.

Now I followed Sheridan's broad back through a landscape quite unlike the one I had expected. Mind you, it suited him. It was a perfect habitat for an old hippie – plenty of sedge, thriving blackberry patch with wattles growing through its centre, rusted-out water tank, fenced dam with four-year-old blue-gum saplings growing around its edge, and beside the cattle pad we walked along, signs of Sheridan's considerable energy – fenced plantings of hakeas, grevilleas, eucalypts. It was not what I had pictured when I imagined a cave in 'the mountains'. I had thought of something deep into the escarpment, a place where you could see the marks where Australia tore itself away from New Zealand.

The cattle pad swung to the left along the contour of a hill but we continued upwards, and there it was – the cave.

It did not look like a cave but a garden shed buried in a hillside. There were plastic buckets everywhere around, and spades and hoes leaning against its windows. It was a cave, of course, with sandstone walls and a great slab of sandstone across its roof. Sheridan with his typical industry had framed out the mouth, building a wall, windows and a door. The result was a big rock-walled room that you could only call cosy. It was a little musty, true, but he quickly laid a fire in his stove. He lit the gas lamp and the refrigerator. He set a kettle on the primus stove. There were two over-stuffed armchairs but I chose to sit on the straight-backed wooden chair behind the desk and looked out through the dusty glass. Far in the distance the light caught the escarpment at Katoomba.

This is where you write?

This book has been a disaster, said Sheridan quietly. It is a total fucking disaster.

I thought you had a publisher.

I do, I do have a publisher.

Congratulations.

No, he said vehemently, I swapped my marriage for a publisher. I came up here for three years and now it is done I haven't got a fucking marriage and all I have is a book. Do you know what she said to me – you burned up all my goodwill. What the fuck does that mean?

But I thought Clara was the one who wanted you to get out of soaps. She thought you were wasting yourself.

Well, she did give that impression, Pete. But while I came up here to write the book she was working eighteen-hour days. She did not complain until she hated me.

That seems unfair.

It's not to do with fair, mate, it's all about her father. I'd kill the fuck if he was not dead already.

I'm sorry, I said.

The truth is, I hate this place now, Pete. I used to be *so* happy when I was here, but now it feels like a tomb.

But you've always loved the mountains.

Yes, he said, I have always loved the mountains. I sort of had the idea that I belonged here.

My brother still farms up towards Lithgow. My grandfather had his first selection in this district. When he was a young fellow he went dancing in a cave not far from here. That was not a cave like this, it was a huge, deep cavern with a proper sprung floor that the cattlemen built. When you see it, you'll marvel at it, the things that men will do for sex. Yes, this is my place, but I should never have written the book. Even if it turns out I have written *Ulysses*, I regret it. I'd rather be writing soaps again. I wouldn't argue with the cunts this time around.

He held out his hand but I did not understand what he wanted.

Give me your tape bloody recorder.

Why?

Why do you think? I'm going to give you your fucking Earth story. He snatched the tape recorder from my hand and, having turned it on, sat beside me at the table.

You know, he said, on the day after she said her goodwill had been burned, I came up to abseil down Danae Canyon.

Let me explain some shit to you. Well, first you know Sydney sandstone is very soft. It's a soft bastard so the creeks cut through it like a knife through butter. You'll have a little creek that started out its life running along at the bottom of a V but over the years it cuts down and it cuts down until the V has become a Y and the shaft of the Y may be only six foot across but it can be hundreds of feet deep and the walls are all eroded in the most beautiful sculpted shapes, and on the sides you'll get hanging gardens of ferns, and spiders and lizards that don't live anywhere else in the world, that have perhaps lived here for a hundred thousand years. It was my mate Skink who got me into this.

The boy who broke his wrists.

They're good fellows, Paul and Skink, and they don't mind a little danger. You look at Skink you wouldn't think he was much, but I've climbed with him and I've fought fires with him and I'd as soon trust my life to him as any man alive. And these canyons can be dangerous, mate. You get caught down one of these holes in a storm you're in deep shit. They're so narrow it doesn't take a lot of water to make them rise. I mean, one minute you could be lying on your back on an airbed, floating down the stream in this gorgeous filtered light and these sculpted golden walls, and the next you could be in a torrent filled with logs and you could die. This is the astonishing thing about Sydney. You drive an hour or two and can go down canyons where no human being has ever been before. Now sometimes these climbs are more in the nature of a picnic, but sometimes we get very serious about it and the time I am speaking about, the day after Clara said, 'My goodwill is all burned up,' four of us had planned to abseil down this amazing waterfall. Danae is a slot down the face of a cliff and the cliff is around two thousand feet.

Two hundred, you mean.

I mean two thousand. I was going to cancel out, I was kind of depressed, but finally I decided that I needed something as big as Danae Canyon to take my mind off my problems. Anyway, the way you do this is go down in a series of what are called 'pitches', steps of fifty metres. You have two ropes tied together, paired. You have these belaying points. No, not bloody pins. Some cowboys will drill holes into the rock and epoxy glue bolts into the rock but I never trusted those. You belay off any solid object – a log, a rock, anything you can put a sling around. You loop your rope through the sling. The point about pairing the ropes is so that you can pull the rope after you when you're at the bottom of each pitch. The sling stays on the belay point. Having done that, however, there's no returning.

Anyway, the first pitch is the most dangerous, because you don't know exactly what conditions you are going to face, and on this occasion I am the first one over. I am halfway down the pitch when I realise the volume of water in this fall is far greater than we had thought. I am wearing a wetsuit but the problem is not getting wet. The thing is, Pete, I cannot fucking breathe. There is a ton of water thundering over me. It is like putting your head out the window of a speeding car.

But it is worse than that. Because there is a fallen tree wedged vertically in the waterfall and when I am halfway down I realise that the rope is caught in the top of the tree, so I am halfway down the pitch and I am out of rope.

Now my mates are waiting on the ledge above me and they can't see me and I push myself out as far as I can and I SCREAM but they can't hear me. And I know that they're going to die on that ledge if I'm stuck, because there is only one rope and I've got it.

So I've got two options. The first, get off the rope and drop, although God knows how far that will be, but to do this I have to disconnect and my weight is holding the release locked tight.

So I climbed the fucking tree. I don't think you can know what it is like to climb a slippery pole against a ton of water. But I manage to do it, and I get the rope free. I am pretty tired and knocked up but I can continue down.

But the fifty-metre rope is insufficient, and I

come to the end with only air beneath me. I am really exhausted by now. I am really sorry I ever started it. No way can I climb that rope against the weight of water. It is not even an option. My only choice is to drop, and hope I don't break my neck. But the damn rope has jammed in the harness, and as long as my weight is on it I cannot release it to drop. I am so weak by now I cannot pull myself up the rope enough to take the weight off the clip in order that it will let go.

And I hung there, and you know I really did not care if I died. In fact, to tell you the truth, death did seem like a pretty good solution, but I could not leave my mates up there. Skink had a one-year-old baby.

So, I gave it one more go. What I had to do, in the middle of this fucking waterfall, was a one-armed chin-up and while I lifted myself in the air with my right hand I fiddled with the harness with the left.

And finally, the sucker opened, and I did not even think: I dropped. I thought, thank Christ it's over. I fell eight feet into a pool five foot deep.

My conversation with Sheridan was in April 2000 and it was a little over six weeks later I received this clipping from the June 15 *Sydney*

Morning Herald. There was no accompanying letter, only a yellow Post-it reading FYI.

Their fatal leap from the edge of the world
By John Huxley

Late-rising kangaroos lingered along the dirt track. Honeyeaters fluttered through the trees. Bushwalkers, some carrying babies on their backs, strode off in search of local attractions such as Mount Cloudmaker, Big Misty and Dance Floor Cave.

And, ever so slowly, the sun climbed over the ridge, burning off the mist and the morning frost.

There is a reassuring familiarity about the Kanangra Falls car park with its discreet toilets, picnic tables and information shelter, all tidily atop Boyd Plateau, high in the Blue Mountains.

But a short walk away – a 'leap off the edge of the world away', as one member of the police rescue squad put it – is an altogether more alien, more hostile environment.

An untamed world. In the words of the National Park guide, 'a labyrinth of creeks, rivers, spiny ridges and deep gorges'.

It was in one of these more remote gorges, near the 400-metre-high Corra Beanga Falls, just five kilometres north-east of the car park, that two members of the Newcastle University Mountaineering Club died last weekend after a three-day expedition went horribly wrong.

It appears the two men were trapped after their ropes became tangled while leading a fifty-metre abseil down the eighth of the thirteen falls that comprise Corra Beanga.

'We believe two ropes were involved,' said Mr Alan Sheehan, of Oberon SES rescue unit. 'The first man made it down and freed his rope. But the second man became tangled in his rope. When the first climbed back up to help him, he too got into trouble.

'It's very rare for ropes to jam. Why did it happen? Maybe we'll never know. Maybe the only two people who know are dead.'

Desperate, torch-lit attempts by their seven colleagues – looking down in horror from forty metres above – to rescue the pair had to be abandoned as night fell and the weather deteriorated.

Forced to spend the night trapped, dangling on the exposed cliff face, lashed by rain, wind and waterfall, Mr Steve Rogers, 26, and Mr Mark Charles, 24, are thought to have died of hypothermia.

'We just don't know, but it could have taken a

matter of minutes. Or a matter of hours,' Mr Sheehan said.

The survivors spent the night on a narrow ledge, barely half a metre wide, shivering, huddled under a flysheet, unable to respond to the cries of help from their friends below.

A senior Chifley police officer, Inspector Peter Thurtell, said it appeared that they did not initially know of the fate of their companions.

'As far as we're concerned, the people that remained up on the ledge above them fully expected to get up in the morning and find their friends camping on the ledge below,' he said.

However, the next morning they realised the worst, and freed their dead friends before starting a three-day slog to safety over what one police rescue squad member described as 'the worst terrain I have ever seen or ever want to see'. They were picked up by a search party, near Kanangra Falls, on Tuesday afternoon.

While the survivors were reunited with family and friends, the grim task of retrieving the bodies resumed in fine, clear weather yesterday.

The two bodies were quickly located, in a pool near the foot of the eighth waterfall, and brought out in two trips by the police rescue helicopter.

The deaths brought to four the number of

people killed in Blue Mountains bushwalking accidents last weekend.

Police and rescue services, however, declined either to criticise the adventurers or to support restrictions on the numbers and types of people using wilderness areas.

CHAPTER EIGHTEEN

THAT NIGHT IN SHERIDAN'S cave I tried to persuade him to tell me about his adventures in the local Volunteer Fire Brigade but no matter how many times he filled his glass he would not soften. I've talked too much already, he said. Ledoux is right, when you've gotten off the hook it's best to be very quiet.

Well let me talk to Skink.

Skink is not a talker, mate, but I'll tell you who is, I'll tell you who is perfect – what's his name, he is married to that gorgeous woman.

You mean Marty Singh, don't you? He lives near here.

How would he get a woman like that? demanded Sheridan.

Well, he's smart. He's attractive.

Attractive, do you really think so?

Sure, and he's curious about everything. He's full of life.

I'm fucking curious, said Sheridan belligerently. Anyway, call the bugger. You need some prize-winning celebrities to liven up this thing. Or ex-celebrities. Either way, he'll talk your leg off. Here, use my mobile phone.

I did ring Marty, and as it turned out he would be happy to tell me about his firefighting adventures but he was leaving the next morning for Broome.

Tape him, hissed Sheridan fiercely. Tape the bastard.

Finally Marty was obliging enough to tape himself and I had nothing to attend to but Sheridan who insisted on pushing his big untidy head against the phone so he could hear the other side of the conversation.

I was, said Marty, down on the coast with Astrid at Bateman's Bay.

That's her, hissed Sheridan, she's fucking gorgeous.

Shut up, Sheridan, said Marty. I was there with Astrid and her mother. Fires were springing up all over Sydney at that time. I don't know what caused them all – lightning, dropped cigarettes.

There was a fucking pyromaniac about, said Sheridan. I don't see how he can say he doesn't know.

Perhaps he's right, sighed Marty. I know one fire was deliberately lit at Mount Wilson. Then, in the town of Colo, a woman had jumped into a swimming pool with her children to escape a fire but they were all killed.

The Mount Wilson fire was not the only one in the Blue Mountains so I telephoned our place just to see what the danger was. We had a couple of friends house-sitting, and I noticed there was a strange tone in their voices. I know they don't scare easily. I mean, these are Tibetan activists who demonstrate in China. But now it seemed they had to rush to Canberra.

Willem, Astrid's brother, was also in the mountains.

Good bloke, said Sheridan.

Willem is an amazing guy, agreed Marty. He'll never panic about anything, he's always so serene and unruffled, but when I asked him about the fires I could hear he was *concerned.*

That's when I knew it was time for me to go. For the first time in our marriage, Astrid packed me a cut lunch! And I set off towards the mountains at 140 kilometres an hour. As I drove I listened to the radio, commercial radio, and I remember hearing the fires on Pittwater were burning right down to the jetty and I knew that meant your old place must have gone. Also that fellow who designed the Aussie dollar notes. His house went. And Dorothy MacKellar's house is right near there, isn't it? You know who I mean, that famous hymn to El Niño! *I love a sunburnt country/A land of sweeping plains*? We were very sunburnt that day, believe me.

There was a police roadblock on the M4. You were only allowed west if you had a mountain address on your driver's licence.

Fuck this, said Sheridan, finally abandoning the tiny phone. I heard a cork pop and then the door slammed shut as he lurched out into the night.

From the plains, Marty continued, all you could see was smoke in the sky and it seemed I was the only car heading west. As I came into the foothills of the mountains I noticed the cars coming towards me had household goods tied on top, towed behind, like refugees. There was absolutely no information on the ABC. There were fires all over Sydney but they had scheduled a broadcast of Arab lesbian quatrains and nothing was going to change their minds.

Meanwhile as I came into the mountains I found ash was falling from the sky. The cars coming round the bends had their headlights on.

An hour later I was at our house, and there was good old Willem. He had already taken down the curtains and was clearing the vegetation back from around the house.

But he had his own place to look out for. So I took over and he went home. It was very, very hot and smoky. Darkness was falling and of course it did not get much cooler. When there was no longer sufficient light to work outside I went up to our tower. There was a ring of fire, burning on the ridges all around. It was really *beautiful*. Can you just imagine – you're up in a tower and through every window, in every direction – fire. At that stage there was no wind and there was no clear indication that it would come up the Grosse Valley, which is our Grand Canyon if you like. So I was not, at that stage, terrified. In fact I had a really good night's sleep.

Next morning it was very hot, hazy with smoke. I dressed in overalls, boots, garden gloves. First I nailed corrugated iron over the skylights. Then I had to make a water dam in the roof gutters. Our house has wide box guttering, and I couldn't block the downpipes with tennis balls like everybody else was doing all over Sydney. I had to be innovative. I found some old dresses of Astrid's – well I thought they were old dresses although it turned out later they were Kenzo – and I wrapped them in plastic and shoved them into the downpipes. Then I flooded the gutters with water. And that's how the day went on, all these fortifications, defences against the fire. I was insanely busy, but not at all unhappy.

And the great thing was, people kept coming in to help. There was an old fellow, Sandy Blake, who was living alone down the road. He came up to help. Then someone brought a chainsaw and dropped a few trees that were hanging too close to the buildings.

Then Willem came back. By this time I'd given up on the radio. There was dense smoke and haze all around us. I didn't need a radio to know I was in the middle of a fire.

The phone lines were all still working and Astrid kept phoning up.

Photo albums!

So I found the fucking photos, which were all of Astrid and her old boyfriends, and I stored them in the laundry which has a double ceiling.

Then the phone was ringing again. My Chinese porcelain!

So I stored her Chinese porcelain.

Then: the wardrobe!

Fuck the wardrobe.

I put some stuff in the laundry and some stuff in the boot of the car but I had no idea what was safe.

By the end of the day, all the things Astrid

cared about were in the laundry covered with
wool blankets. The gutters were brimful of water.
There were also buckets of water everywhere. But
what do you do with videotapes? I had tapes of
all my animation, every foot of film I had ever
produced, and videotapes are like little barrels of
oil, the most explosive things of all.

Early evening on this second day, I got a call
from a niece who works in National Parks. She
was phoning from a helicopter: Marty, I'm over
your way now. The fire's coming up on Govern-
or's. That was close, only a few miles down the
end of our road.

Then I got a call from a neighbour who said
he'd seen fire trucks going up towards my place.

I'd just hung up when all these volunteer firefighters came bursting into my house. There were
a couple of guys I recognised, including the guy
from the local garage. Marty, he said, we need tea
towels.

So I gave them my tea towels.

We've got to get you out of here, Marty.

They wet the towels and tore them up and
wrapped them round their faces but they could
not hide their panicked eyes. I don't want to
demean these volunteers. They were very brave
and they were very helpful to me. But those eyes
were scary to behold.

We've got orders. You've got to be evacuated.

I don't need to be evacuated.

No, no, don't give us any trouble, Marty.

So where's the captain?

But they had already escorted old Sandy Blake out to the car. And I was next. I didn't want to be an arsehole but I was absolutely livid. I was thinking, they can't do this to me. We were escorted in a convoy, and as we were driving down the road there were more fire trucks coming towards my house.

The convoy drove for about ten minutes to the point where the dirt road meets the asphalt road which the locals call 'The Rink'. This was now basecamp for the firefighting units – fire trucks, cop cars, my neighbours. You couldn't see a hundred yards. There was a feeling of panic.

Then I discovered I didn't have my wallet.

I've left my wallet behind, I said to the cop.

Any guy understands this. A man must have his wallet.

I've got to go back and get it.

All right, Marty, he said, I'll see if I can get permission.

Come on, I said, we don't need permission.

All right, get in the bloody car.

As I was getting into the car, who did I see, talking his way through the roadblock? It was

Willem. So this young cop drives us both through the smoke and ash back to my house.

By now the place is swarming with firefighters, but they didn't have the outside lights on and they couldn't find my water tanks.

I've got to stay. These fellows don't know where anything is.

Finally this young cop gives in.

The firefighters had a map which showed the contours of the land between our house and Governor's Rest, but they were having trouble reading it.

They were asking how many valleys there were between my place and Governor's.

Well, said Willem, the first one's here.

And straight away there was order. As Willem briefed them on the land my living room became like a war room.

By this time poor old Sandy Blake had been taken off and spent a hideous night in a boarding house. But I was in my home with my brother-in-law, who helped build the house and was very confident about its ability to withstand the fire. Mind you, I also had these guys with my tea towels wrapped around their faces. What was that about? I asked them. Why were you evacuating me?

Mate, we've been fighting bushfires for twenty

years and we never saw anything like that. We were down on Governor's Rest and we never seen flames like that, not ever.

Anyway, everything was calmer now. I showed them where my tanks of water were. I had a *lot* of water. And they brought a tanker very close. I showed them the tracks and dirt roads. I showed them the other buildings and we made decisions about what was to be sacrificed and what was to be fought for. The main house was most important, then that building, then that one, and so on. We turned the outside lights on.

At about one in the morning the winds slowed down a bit and I was informed that we were going to need to back-burn. And then these guys came out of the dark with these things like watering cans and I watched as they poured liquid fire on to the ground. They just wandered round, in big fucking circles, setting my garden alight. Holy shit. Now I had two rings of fire, a close one and a distant one. And, yes, it was a little scary. I was running around saying, no, not that tree, because I was trying to stop the oak trees being burnt – the Aussie trees will replenish after fire, but the English oaks will die.

Then, suddenly, the house lights went off.

I asked the National Parks guy, what happened with the power?

Oh we cut it off.

Why would you do that?

We're doing a back-burn.

Yes but if you turn the power off my water pumps won't work.

Agh, he said. Nothing ever goes simply, does it?

So now I had no bloody power. And I had these new fires close around my house. Naturally, I was feeling a lot more vulnerable.

There were a lot of experienced firefighters but also some who were in training. There were twenty or thirty guys, chainsaws singing right through the night, lots of rakes, shovels, containing this back-burn.

Then, suddenly, it's dawn, and they're packing up their chainsaws, drifting back towards their trucks.

And suddenly I'm left alone, with no power, no hoses, and all this smouldering bush, these flaming stumps surrounding me. Also our pine trees are big, fifty or sixty years old, and the fire has gone underground and is, without me knowing it, quietly burning along their roots.

And the winds, as they say, become 'variable'. The spot fires began to come up everywhere and all I had were buckets of water to put them out.

There was a roadblock in the street, so none of

my friends could reach me, except for Willem who could always get through a roadblock.

So that was my life that week, and it didn't alter when the power came on. Hardly any sleep. Constantly putting out these fires. Not even answering the phone. Not being terrified, but staying very, very alert.

And then, said Marty, another fire was coming from the east, from Wombat Rock.

So I started chainsawing back the bush around the hut where Astrid has her pottery.

Then people did start to turn up, with food, helping to beat back the fire with wet sacks. Willem came and went often. Some others came and fled. You know the old days when people came to watch wars? It became a little like that.

There was a rooster in the house and a pet rabbit. And at this stage they suddenly became very domesticated and friendly. You can't have an Aussie story without a chook in it, can you? So here it is, accompanied by a rabbit. I went down to the tree house, they came with me.

The sky was scarlet. It was hard to breathe. Behind my back the fire was raging down Spy Hill. So there was only a road between me and Spy Hill. And the noise! You could hear it crackling, roaring. The sound was completely terrifying. Also the fire was shooting out flaming debris in advance, so all this burning ordnance is falling from the sky.

And that was when I thought, I could die. And here is the thing, the big thing for me. I felt that was all right. I didn't curl up in the foetal position.

I walked away from the house, down towards the escarpment, and began to deal with spot fires there. Somewhere about this point my sister Jodie and her boyfriend came to bring me some food.

And they looked at the fire on Spy Hill and they looked at this mad ash-black fellow whacking at the bush with a wet sack. And they said, *Marty*, it's time to get out of here.

But no way was I going to leave.

Marty.

You go if you have to. That's fine.

And they pissed off so fucking quick. For a while it was just me and the rabbit and the chook.

But soon enough my friend Leon arrived all kitted up with the proper overalls and boots. Next came old Sandy Blake. It was obvious he wasn't well. His hands were all puffed up, like rubber gloves full of water. He started picking up big logs and clearing them away.

Sandy, you shouldn't be doing that.

Bullshit, he said, I want to be useful.

And we were there, the three of us, beating the

flames with our wet sacks. And suddenly I realised this was kind of nice.

At that moment we were true neighbours, fighting the fire side by side. And it felt very good to be alive.

Isn't he finished yet? cried Sheridan, bursting into the cave and collapsing on one of the overstuffed chairs where he promptly fell asleep.

Marty paused. What's that noise, Peter?

Sheridan. He's asleep now.

Agh, poor old Sheridan, said Marty. Did he tell you about the kid who broke both his wrists?

Yes.

And about Danae Canyon?

Yes.

One word of advice, Peter.

Yes?

Don't talk to him about firestick farming. It drives him nuts.

CHAPTER NINETEEN

I WAS WOKEN BY the rush of coffee from an espresso and a loud grating noise like a rusty hinge.

Move your arse, called Sheridan, and I lifted myself up on my elbows, not too far, because this ledge at the back of the cave had a three-foot ceiling, and peered out through the grey feathery scrub. The rusty hinge grated again.

Red-tailed black cockatoos, explained Sheridan. He was standing at the table hacking into last night's lamb.

You already missed the kangaroos. They've been and gone. Come on, mate, we've got to get back to the city.

Looking around the cave I saw that almost everything we had carried from the car had been once more packed away. Beside the lamb was a cardboard box and a bulging garbage bag.

What's the rush?

Well, mate, you weren't coming to see me, let's face it.

Oh Jesus, Sherry. Don't talk like that.

I'm not hurt. It's true. I know you're a working writer. You're trying to get old Jack to tell you his story. That's OK, he said, but his eyes were dark and glistening and he turned to the espresso and filled two mugs.

Sheridan, how do you know that?

Sheridan placed the brimming coffee on the table. He's my friend too, he said reproachfully. I talked to him. You want some of this lamb before we leave?

I shook my head and Sheridan, having carved himself one final bloody slice, threw the remainder into a plastic bag.

Jack's going to tell you the story, he announced. You're meeting him at Bar Coluzzi for lunch. You better move your arse if you plan on getting back to town in time.

Ten minutes later we were carrying the bag and box through the wet grass to the car. Here I watched Sheridan take a long swallow of coffee, survey the gloomy sky belligerently, empty the remainder of his coffee on the ground, stand his mug upside down on a fence post.

That's that, he said, throwing the lamb on to the back seat.

Do you get lonely up here? I asked him.

No time to get lonely, mate. Too bloody busy.

Yet all this energy looked dangerous to me. I worried about Sheridan and remembered his book on homeless men, the winos, the derros of Darlinghurst. In half the biographies Sheridan had so lovingly collected, the hinge, the pivot of their lives, would be the moment when 'the missus died' or 'she kicked me out'. You would like to think that self-knowledge had led him to these men, but that was not his strong card, as Clara would soon be telling anyone who wished to listen.

Sheridan had the engine going before I was in the car.

Listen to that, he said. He gave the accelerator a quick pump. Bloody beautiful.

Didn't you have something you wanted to do out here?

Nah, he said. No ties, mate, free as a bird.

He was sitting up high peering over the wheel, looking out for threatening rocks, but once we were on the road he relaxed.

I'll have you at Bar Coluzzi in an hour and a half. This is a fabulous cruising car.

The story would be neater if the explosion

came just then, but it arrived no more than twenty minutes later, on the outskirts of Blackheath. The noise was enormous. I felt it in my gut and the Merc lurched, shuddered, and came to a violent stop.

Quick, said Sheridan as black smoke began to rise from beneath the hood. Get out of the car, quick.

Later I understood that he had imagined the engine was on fire, but at the time I took exception to being pulled out of the car so forcefully. Traffic was threading its way around the smoking Merc but still he would not release me, gripping my forearm as I tried to struggle free.

A minute or two later Sheridan announced that there was no longer any danger of explosion. He insisted I push the injured vehicle off the road and there, having first warned me to step well back, he slowly lifted the hood.

My own brother was trained as a motor mechanic and he tells me he never saw a thing like this in forty years: the wall of the engine block looked as if it had been hit by an armour-piercing shell – there was a jagged hole about three inches wide.

I'm fucked, said Sheridan.

He did not mean that the repair was beyond his means. His life was fucked. There would be no good luck any more, and when a tow truck pulled in behind us Sheridan looked at it mulishly for a moment before giving it the benefit of his broad back. The driver, a slender olive-skinned woman of perhaps thirty-five, came to join us, tucking in her plaid shirt as she walked.

Jesus, she said. That's ugly.

Thanks a fucking million, said Sheridan.

She shrugged and walked around the car.

You watch this, Sheridan muttered. She's going to offer me fifty bucks to take it off my hands. I hate these fucking vultures.

If she heard him she gave no sign of it. She jerked her head towards the mess of books amongst the climbing gear. You a teacher?

No.

You read books?

What do you think?

I read too, the tow-truck driver said, so focused on the books that she did not seem to notice any rudeness. Not much else to do up here, she said.

It took this long for Sheridan to begin to understand that he was, if not exactly being hit on, then at least having the ground prepared so he could hit on her. He brushed his hair back out of his eyes and squinted at her. I'm a writer, he declared.

In unconscious imitation she pulled her hair

back off her own face then quickly turned to peer into the car. You would not say she was a beauty but she was young and she had such clear unprotected eyes.

That's not your book in there, is it? All those pages.

Parts of it, admitted Sheridan.

He's not shitting me? she frowned at me earnestly. He really is a writer?

He's not shitting you.

You can see what's happening here. Before ten more minutes had passed she had run to the cab of her truck and shown him her battered copy of Russell Hoban's *Riddley Walker* and he had read her the opening paragraph from his manuscript. And then she offered to drive us to inspect a Merc engine in a wrecker's yard in Lithgow.

It's up to you, Pete, he said.

Why me?

You'll miss your meeting with Jack.

It took an hour to get to Lithgow and there was no sign of a Mercedes there. Neither of them seemed to give a damn. Vicki (that was her name) gunned the truck back down the highway to All-Star Wrecking outside Katoomba and all this time the pair of them shouted at each other over the roar of the engine. You never heard two people who had so many books in common and Sheridan was no longer belligerent and hurt but charming, curious, solicitous. I could not know if he was sincere or was just one more cattleman building a dance floor so he could get laid.

When he shook hands with me outside the Katoomba railway station I noticed his wedding ring had miraculously disappeared. He followed my glance.

I'm separated, he said. I told you.

CHAPTER TWENTY

AND NOT A PEEP to him about the firestick, said the all-too-familiar voice. You are far too obedient to be in this line of work.

You would prefer me to torment my friend, I said sarcastically, provoking a sharp glance from the carriage's only other inhabitant. This natty gent was tucked up in the corner with his *Sporting Globe*. He wore a shiny suit and a colourful tweed hat such as are favoured by the racing fraternity.

Has it ever occurred to you, my invisible companion continued, that for a timid person you have a high percentage of friends who are hanging off ropes or getting themselves killed in some dangerous hobby? There is something very psychological in this. You are far too timid.

You think me frightened of Sheridan? I enquired.

You would be wise to be afraid of him, but I know why you did not mention the old firestick.

Why?

You are scared to death of it, there is no question.

And why would that be, do you imagine?

If you confront the indigenous people's ways of using fire, you will have to stop promoting them as children of nature.

It is not up to me to promote anyone as anything.

In any case, the evidence is heavily against such a pretty thought. The day they arrive they are at it with their fires. Smoke, smoke, always burning. Thank Christ they didn't come with bulldozers.

Ah, you should read Flannery.

I have read far more of Flannery than you have of de Selby and I will prove it. Flannery says that they wiped out all the big slow friendly animals. They are like the Maoris in New Zealand who exterminated the moa in a hundred years. They killed them in their thousands, only eating their legs and haunches. That was not at all ecological, you'll agree. They killed so many moas that they quickly reduced themselves to starvation and cannibalism. Take some advice, you will do far better if you allow the Aboriginals are human just like us.

Shut up a moment, I cried, and the racing gent folded up his newspaper and, without so much as a look in my direction, walked into the connecting carriage.

He's off to report you to the authorities.

I will not say the Aboriginals did not affect the landscape.

Of course not. How could you? But once you allow that the Aboriginals might have caused actual damage to the soil, then that weakens you with the loggers and the mining companies. That's the heart of it. That's why you're frightened of firestick farming.

You could not be more wrong. If they farmed with fire, they farmed. They tended the land. This is what the British would never allow . . .

Here's the conductor.

. . . and if it is true then it makes the occupation of the land not only cruel but illegal.

The conductor gave me a piercing look, clipped my ticket very carefully, and returned it to me without a word.

CHAPTER TWENTY-ONE

AS EVERY TAX ACCOUNTANT must concede, you cannot write about Water without eating fish and you cannot get better fish in Sydney than at Neil Perry's Rockpool Restaurant and that was where Kelvin and I were, eating the most perfectly tax-deductible pearl perch, when Clara phoned. I still have not figured out how she knew I was there.

She rang to say that she had just seen Sheridan, who had accused her of stealing his Vietnam service medals, and she was seriously worried about his mental balance. She thought he was with their youngest son in a squat down at the bottom of Sussex Street and she begged me to go and find him.

But Clara had to wait on the phone for five minutes because there was a third diner at the table and he would not let his story be interrupted. Fix Neal was a big man, bigger, wider, heavier than Kelvin. He had a thick neck and powerful hands, and his eyes were small and blue and filled with a fast quizzical intelligence.

Not yet, he told the waiter.

He was telling a story about a conference in the mountain town of Tumut with characters who we will simply refer to by their public titles: the premier and the attorney general.

So we were all there, he said, and he named the famous names. And we took over the pub for the conference and when we had finished all the serious shit we took over the bar and at one in the morning the poor bloody publican comes out.

Time, gentlemen, please.

Everyone ignores him so he goes to the premier and tells him I'll lose my licence if I stay open.

So the premier looks him up and down. You wouldn't want him to look at you like that, Peter. He could be very charming, as you know, but he was a hard bastard.

Where's your licence? he asks the publican.

Over there, behind the bar.

The licence is all properly framed and 'clearly displayed' as the law demands.

Give it to me.

The publican hesitates but then he lifts the frame off its hook and gives it to the premier who smashes it down on the bar. Glass goes everywhere.

Hey, Bawbles, the premier calls to the attorney general. Hey, Bawbles, have you got a pen, mate?

Yes, mate.

Well endorse this gentleman's licence, will you.

So the attorney general removes the official paper from the shattered frame and he lays it carefully on a nice dry part of the bar. Then he writes: 'These premises are permitted to remain open from midnight until six am.' And he dates it and signs his name – so and so, attorney general.

And everyone stays up drinking half the night.

The next day as we're all leaving, the premier turns to me as I get in the car.

Did you get that licence back, Fix?

She's fixed, mate. She's sweet.

He laughed. He was the fixer. He had fixed it. We all laughed. And this is the thing that I perhaps should not confess – we *liked* this reckless behaviour. We liked the lawlessness and if we sometimes suspected our leaders were a little criminal then they were our criminals at least.

That's Sydney, mate, said Fix, that's Sydney to a fucking tee. It's a hard place.

Sir, said the waiter at last.

It's a very hard place, continued Fix. And he was a hard bastard, he had to be to be premier.

He said to me once, after someone had stabbed him in the back. He said, I don't know why he shafted me, I never did him a favour. You see, Peter? You understand? The fellow who accepts the favour is weakened by it.

Sir? said the waiter.

Get the fuck out of here, said the aggressively heterosexual Fix, flirting and threatening simultaneously.

The waiter was tall and slender and very, very handsome. He looked Fix up and down, rumpled shirt, bulging belly. Telephone, he said evenly.

God knows what was said while I spoke to Clara, but five minutes later I had paid the bill and we were out in the drizzling rain. Fix had left the table reluctantly and now he was trying to persuade us not to visit the squat.

You don't know what it is, he said. You don't know what sort of vermin are there. Is this the junkie son or the Captain Planet son?

It's Captain Planet, said Kelvin, but I'll tell you honestly, Fix, I don't see that we have a choice.

And that was how it came about, as the rain began on the night before Anzac Day, that three middle-aged men found themselves climbing through the ground-floor window of a building that has since been demolished. The stairs smelled bad. They were very dark and made almost impassable by stacked window sashes, filing cabinets, office partitions and God knows what else. On the fifth-floor landing the floor-boards had been removed and we could only continue to the roof, where Sheridan was said to be inhabiting the caretaker's apartment, by walking across a single plank.

This is a very stupid thing to be doing, said Fix.

It occurred to me then that my companions, being both large men in rumpled suits, looked very like cops and the thought did not comfort me.

CHAPTER TWENTY-TWO

WE FOUND THE SQUAT up on the roof of the eight-storey building, a former caretaker's residence like a suburban fibro shed. Sherry's six-foot son was standing in the open doorway.

Dad, come in out of the rain. Light shone across the wet black roof and revealed the hairy shirtless Sheridan kneeling on the slippery parapet looking down into the night.

Dad? Like a barefoot surfer crossing a painful car park, the boy hobbled out into the rain. He had his Dutch mother's long narrow feet and sand-white hair.

What is it that you see, Dad?

Sheridan's hair and beard were wet and matted. He pointed along the lines of rain. Chook, he said.

His son put his arm around his father's naked

shoulder and the two of them peered down together.

Do you know why we call a chicken a chook? asked Sheridan. It's from the Gaelic, did you know that?

As we watched, a woman appeared in the door-way. She had a scarf around her head and a sarong tucked in between her breasts. I did not know her until she spoke but when I heard that throaty voice I recognised Vicki the tow-truck driver. What are you buggers up to? she demanded.

As she came towards the parapet Sheridan quickly rose to intercept, but she feinted, ducked beneath his widespread arms, and discovered what so interested the blond boy.

Oh, she cried in distress. Oh no. My chook.

She's alive, said Sherry as he joined her. She's not hurt.

Oh you're such a fucking expert, Sherry, cried Vicki as she turned to face him. I don't know why I trusted you.

Sheridan began to pat the air.

Sweetheart, I'll rescue her, no worries. You've got to trust me, please.

You're such an old con, Vicki cried. You stay away from her.

Oh Jesus, don't say that, pleaded Sheridan, you don't know what it does to me.

It was at this delicate moment that Fix led us forward.

Hello Fix, said Sheridan. He nodded to me and Kelvin before turning to stare down off the edge. There, by the light of the red flashing sign on the Cho-How Dumpling House, I could see what appeared to be a crumpled ball of rag on the grimy window ledge a floor below. It was a chook.

Dad, you're pissed, said Jason. You can't go down the rope while you're pissed.

I never said anything about a rope.

And a bottle of wine, said Jason. Please, mate, don't do this to me.

Everyone went very quiet.

All right, said Fix. Can a bloke make a suggestion?

Who the fuck is he? Vicki demanded.

I'm Fix, darling, and I am very fucking well named.

He took the little plastic bucket of grain from Sheridan's hands. Get me some string.

While the son went inside, Fix produced a Swiss army knife with which he made some holes in the tub. The son then returned with a ball of twine which Fix cut and then threaded through the holes.

Vicki watched, her arms folded across her breasts.

Peter Carey

You expect the chook to jump in that? she asked.

Fix revealed the same smile I had seen him bestow on the waiter at the Rockpool. Observe, he said.

This won't work, Kelvin whispered. He's pissed.

You shut the fuck up, said Fix.

I was the one who knelt beside him as he lowered the container down the northern edge of the light-well. On the southern side, the others huddled in the light rain, their pale faces washed red by the flashing sign.

Stop, called Sheridan. You're just above her. Drop it maybe six inches.

Four inches.

Her head is in it, said Jason. She's pecking.

Pull it now, you won't get another chance.

Don't pull.

Jesus, said Fix, tugging on the line. Stand by, Pete.

She's going to fall, cried Vicki.

I was kneeling on the parapet, not a good place for the vertiginous.

She's going to fucking fall.

I was wearing the trousers of the suit I had bought at Barney's in New York but there did not seem any choice but to lie down on the filthy roof. And here came the chook, like a wound-up spring, head down, arse in the air. It was only momentum that kept her pinned in place and as she ascended, swaying, bouncing against the wall, she was struggling to straighten herself. I clenched my teeth, reached towards her and as I did so she launched herself. I grabbed, missed, then caught her foot.

I crawled backwards, dragging her to safety, and as I rolled she struck, driving her beak into my wrist.

Shit!

The chook rose free, flapped towards the edge of death, then went running across the roof towards the compost heap, leaving me alone with blood pouring down across my open palm.

To my great irritation I found Fix was laughing at me. See, he said, see. Comrade Chook.

Shut up, Fix.

You did the comrade a favour, she had to peck you. She's a Sydney chook, no worries.

Very funny, I said.

Come on, he said, pulling me to my feet. Do you think old Captain Planet might have a toke of Mary Jane?

CHAPTER TWENTY-THREE

SOME OF THE MOST extraordinary places in which I have lived have been sited on land occupied by people popularly known as dole bludgers. I am thinking particularly of my years in Browns Creek Road, Yandina which was not exactly a commune but was certainly a hippie community. Here I dwelled on the edge of rain-forest in a beautiful little hut and all around my neighbours tended their gardens in the cool of the morning and, in the hot afternoons, swam in a rock pool above a waterfall. I am not saying it was perfect, but even when we were burdened with the harassment of the Nambour building inspector or frightened by the threats of the notorious Queensland drug squad, we only had to drive half an hour to find the long peaceful beaches of the Sunshine Coast.

Up and down the east coast of Australia various friends of mine have lived similar (not exactly untroubled) lives but always in the midst of a beauty you could not have improved on, not even with paid employment.

However it was not until I walked across the roof of that squat and discovered all of Darling Harbour spread beneath me, that the penny finally dropped – hippies and their successors have a great nose for real estate. This was a million-dollar location.

There was a kind of verandah or balcony on the western side of the caretaker's flat. Jason and a temporarily absent character named Moosh had paved its floor with an abstract mosaic of broken plates and tiles. Their work was now pushing up the walls where it was morphing into a bright blue and yellow depiction of a sandy cove. On the balcony was a big white plastic table (which looked like something by Saarinen) and eight slightly shop-soiled red vinyl chairs discarded by the Cho-How Dumpling House. The squatters had made something you might be delighted to find on a beach in Queensland or Bali, although this illusion was challenged by the high ugly yellow-brick building just across the way. The owners of these expensive apartments may or may not have been amazed by the chook and/ or the organic farmers on the rooftop below them. Jason, of course, was *certain* that they were *continually* amazed. He hugged himself and scratched his tanned biceps in delight.

You should see them, mate, he said. You come here at seven o'clock at night. They're all talking on their mobile phones, looking down at us. Just imagine what is going on inside their brains!

Captain Planet! He never doubted that his compost caused immense unease amongst his yuppie neighbours.

And if he wished to challenge his enemies he could not have found a better place to do it, for in all of Sydney it would have been hard to find a stronger reminder of the dazzling strength of his opposition. Their power was here laid out before him in a sight that was not merely *awful*, but *awful* elevated to a giddy height and sickening width, a panorama of *awful*, a chaotic, anarchic *awful* of such exuberance and density that it was (not quite, but almost) beautiful.

It was this shoreline growth that the ugly monorail was built to feed, so we might suffer this encrustation on a stretch of harbour which another city might have thought to treat as lungs, a way to bring the air and water deep into the city heart.

Here the polluticians and the developers carved up the cake with gusto. It is not hard to imagine that every one of them was determined to do something unique. They built structures with soaring roofs like tents, glowing blue cones that would have been science fiction twenty years before. It was on the shores of Chinatown. So they made Chinese gardens, funfairs, aquariums. It was Coney Island with fine dining. It was the bastard child of Corbusier and Ronald McDonald. It was the twenty-first century with the Jetsons zooming past in the monorail on their way to eat John Dory and drink a glass – make that a bottle – of cold white wine. The curse of Botany Bay was gone. Here was the proof – this was the arsehole of the world no more.

And it had, once, been the cloaca, the dump, the port, filthy water, tanneries, warehouses and factories, and the developers no doubt feel they have improved it out of sight. Have they not kept those Georgian warehouses on the western shore? And anyway, no matter what Jason and his friends might say, there was no conspiracy. Yes Laurie Brereton, a minister in the state Labor government, pushed through that monorail with such determination that it would not have mattered how many Nobel Prize winners had marched beside us through the streets, no citizen could stop this thing. It was a conspiracy, said Jason, but a conspiracy requires a plan, and this was more of a Rum Corps goldrush. That high-cabled bridge over there was not designed by anyone connected with, say, the Panasonic IMAX just by the waterfront. Yes, it has a similar funfair aspect to it, a similar liveliness, a vibrancy, an energy – are they bad things? That the Police Witness Protection Programme should be neighbour to the IMAX, that it should have opaque-glass windows like a drug-dealer's limo, that it snuggles comfortably against the monorail, perhaps means no more than this is a city as organic as a coral reef, all its denizens bunching in intimate complexity. Perhaps we should pray that the Central Business District should finally attain this same mass of exhibitionistic awfulness, this density of domes, cones, freeways, bridges, fantasy, and when it finally does it will give off a luminous exotic energy, like the streets of *Blade Runner* without, God willing, the rain to wreck our summer.

Jason, it was obvious, was very proud of his home. He made a very tasty guacamole dip and brought cold beer to the table.

I asked him if he thought the view was beautiful.

It's pretty fucked, eh? But the way he grinned and rested his feet up on the parapet seemed celebratory as much as critical. It's a ringside seat, he said.

It's terrifying, Vicki said. If she had been angry with Sheridan about the chook, all that had vanished.

What are you terrified of, Vicki? Fix's voice had an edge to it. She was friendly towards him but he (*Who the fuck is he?*) had taken a set against her.

We should all be terrified, said Jason quickly. You look at this development and you can imagine what they'll do to Cockatoo Island now it's up for grabs.

They? asked Fix, raising his eyebrows. Who the fuck is *they?*

Sheridan leaned forward and laid his hand on Vicki's shoulder, all the while addressing Fix. We know you worked for Laurie Brereton, mate. But we don't blame you personally.

Fix narrowed his eyes. Maybe THEY will build an opera house, he said. You people are such fucking knee-jerks. You've got no idea what it takes to get things done.

Jack Ledoux is working on plans for developing Cockatoo Island, said Kelvin. That has to be a plus.

Oh come on, Kelvinator, groaned Fix. Jack's an artist, mate.

Vicki cocked her head and stared at this wide heavy man with the white shirt and loosened tie. You make that sound so dirty, she said. You make me shiver when you say it.

Sweetheart, I've known Jack for twenty years. He's a sweet fellow but he's a wanker. No government's going to let him decide how to develop a billion dollars' worth of real estate.

If it was Utzon you'd be calling *him* a wanker.

Fix snorted into his beer. Look, you're all so critical of everything. You look down at Darling Harbour and say, oh, how awful. How UNAESTHETIC. But you tell me, Jason, why are you living here? I'll tell you why? This is a fabulous view. It's a sensational place. And yes, I know, it's fucked, Jason, but it's a city, mate, and it's exciting. It's a world-class city and the only cities you like are really country fucking towns.

Look, said Jason, that is Cockle Bay down there. Doesn't that tell you something is lost? It doesn't have much to do with cockles any more.

Oh Jesus, save me from the eco-left! exclaimed Fix and held his head in his hands.

Go easy, mate, said Kelvin.

You know something, Jason? I am sick and fucking tried of hearing about the Abos' midden heaps, mate, no offence.

Sheridan shifted uncomfortably and put his hand on Vicki's arm. That's her mob, he said quickly.

I turned, suddenly, to look at Vicki and she caught me and held my gaze. Didn't figure me for a blackfellow? she said.

No, I didn't.

But we are everywhere amongst you, she sipped her beer. Reading *books,* driving *tow trucks.*

Come on, said Sheridan, Peter's cool.

Oh I'm cool too, said Vicki bitterly. I'm a real truck-driving, post-modernist Koori.

So where's your country, Vicki? Fix asked, his blue eyes sparkling.

Shut up, said Sheridan. She doesn't have a bloody country. It was stolen from her.

I can speak for myself, thanks, Sherry, and I do have a country, Fix. It's up near Moree.

She was taken from her parents, explained Sherry.

Vicki cast a fast hard look on Sheridan which made it very clear that this information was not his to give away. She seemed about to speak, then changed her mind.

In the embarrassed hiatus that followed Kelvin fetched more beers and Vicki rolled a cigarette. Then we all watched an ambulance make its way into the city over the Western Distributor.

Listen, Vicki said at last, I don't want to talk about this shit.

I did not bring this up, said Fix.

Vicki cocked her head and studied him with her intense dark eyes. You can't bring up something that is always there. But the minute you discover I'm a Koori you're not going to say, oh, what do you think of David Malouf's new novel? You're going to go, oh, where's your country, as if you knew what that meant.

I apologise, said Fix.

Vicki nodded and stroked her forehead. She had a small single frown line just above her nose. See, I've got a white mum just like you have. I've got a white dad, a real old digger, I marched with him each Anzac Day until he died. But I grew up not knowing I had a black mum and a black dad. I did not even know I was a Koori, and now it seems that has to be the only interesting thing about me.

I didn't mean that, said Fix.

That's all right, don't worry. She stood and picked up her pouch of tobacco and her matches.

Tomorrow is Anzac Day. Sherry and I have to get up for the Dawn Service.

Can I come with you? asked Fix suddenly.

Suit yourself, said Vicki. And disappeared inside.

CHAPTER TWENTY-FOUR

COULD MY EIGHTEEN-YEAR-OLD self have seen me at the Dawn Service on Anzac Day he would, if he had not wept with disappointment, have jeered and shouted slogans at the man he would become.

In the eyes of that eighteen year old, Anzac Day was celebrated by men who hated Asians and loved the Queen of England, racists, royalists, homophobes, soldiers in uniform who saw his long hair as an enemy badge. Anzac Day meant the Returned Services League and RSL clubs, and that single minute of every alcoholic day when a dreary male voice intoned LEST WE FORGET and the beer ceased flowing and the poker machines fell silent in tribute to the dead.

I might have mocked and feared the reactionary RSL but even as an opinionated teenager I knew the issue was more complicated. My heart was easily stirred by the story of Gallipoli. My own father had fought in neither world war but we had family friends who had suffered the Burmese Railway, Changi Prison and the horrors of the Kokoda Trail. The road into our little town was lined with a massive avenue of plane trees, each bearing the name of a local boy or man who had lost his life in war. It was the most beautiful place in the entire town and one could not drive through it and not think why it was there. 'The Japanese,' my mother said, 'were coming to take my little baby.' Why would I not believe her? Had I not, in the grounds of State School No. 28, played with the currency the Japanese had printed in readiness for the time when our country would be theirs? Did we not dance home along the footpaths chanting *Step on a crack and break a Jap's back*?

But then came the 1960s and Vietnam and the RSL was still fighting the same old Asian war, and we heard their fear and hatred of the Japanese and could see nothing more complicated than their racism. At eighteen I was becoming aware of some of my country's bloodier secrets. I joined protest marches against the Vietnam War and the White Australia policy. Aboriginal activists like Charles Perkins were continuing the long fight for human rights for black Australians.

In this climate, Australia was bitterly divided, and the RSL, the guardians and administrators of the Anzac Day march, stood on the right. Their members were the mythic diggers but now they were my enemy. I could not see that they were also me. I did not know that history is like a bloodstain that keeps on showing on the wall no matter how many new owners take possession, no matter how many times we paint over it.

Year after year the old diggers pinned on their medals, and at four thirty in the morning, at the hour the Australian and New Zealand army corps was landing on the Turkish coast, they laid their wreaths on their dreary monuments to the war dead, and then they marched and later they drank and for many of them the marching turned to staggering as they wandered bellicose or sentimental through the streets. We had no idea of what they'd seen and done and now we did not want to know. They were the old Australia, white men with names like Smith and Bennett and Kelly and McGrath, and each year they grew older and we waited for the time when the last of them would die and then, we imagined, Anzac Day would wither and nothing would remain but some dreary statues in country towns and that great granite cenotaph in Martin Place. Korea, of course, supplied a few new marchers, and Vietnam topped up the crowd, but by the year 2000, on that morning when Vicki had parked her station wagon in Bligh Street, there were only thirty-one survivors of the battle against the Turks at Gallipoli. I was fifty-seven, finally old enough to honour them.

Kelvin looked slumped and miserable, as you might expect of a married man who had stayed out all night and now had no reasonable explanation for his behaviour. Fix and I did not look a whole heap better, but Sheridan was dressed in a neat black suit with two Vietnam medals on his breast. I had never seen these medals before. I was not surprised he had them, only that he wore them. My attitude towards Sherry's Vietnam service had been shaped, long, long ago, during all those smelly hours he had held his feet to the radiator, spreading the bright pink rash he was sure would save him from the draft.

Beside him walked Vicki in a crisp black suit, her foster father's raft of medals pinned across her breast. On her right lapel she wore a large Aboriginal Land Rights badge.

It was still before dawn when I realised that Anzac Day was not something that had withered. There were teenagers here, young couples in their

twenties, so many of them that although we had
risen at half past three we could not even push
our way into Martin Place. We could not see the
cenotaph or the dignitaries who presided over the
event.

In 1967 Fix had gone to jail for burning his
draft card. Kelvin and I had been too old to face
the lottery but he had been an active member of
the Vietnam Moratorium Committee in Sydney
(just as I had in Melbourne). I don't know exactly
what my friends felt now, but I was certainly
ready to make peace with our past.

Then I looked down at the printed programme.
And what I felt will seem unreasonable, I'm sure.

0430 hrs. MC Leon Becker AM.

Hymn: Abide With Me.

Prayer: Senior Chaplain.

*Address: Commander Blah Blah Blah. The
Patron: His Excellency, the Honourable Gordon
Samuels AC, Governor of NSW, will recite ded-
ication.*

Everything about this language depressed me.
It was like going into a lift in an old building and
detecting the odour of Bakelite in the light fix-
tures, the smell of Australia in 1955.

Will recite dedication.

Oh charmless people!

His Excellency, the Honourable.

Kissers of royal arses!

The Patron will place the wreath of the Australian Legion on the Cenotaph. Official representatives will immediately follow.

Oh nation of postmasters and accountants, is this our greatest story? Are our poets in prison?

As the dawn is even now about to pierce the night so let their memory inspire us to work for the coming new light into the dark places of the world.

What new light? I thought as I listened to that dull dreary voice on the PA. What dark places did they mean?

The Patron will place the wreath of the Australian Legion on the Cenotaph.

And then, incredibly, the band struck up 'God Save the Queen'.

Jesus, whispered Fix. Not that.

Shut up, said Vicki fiercely. Her eyes were glistening. We shut up. But Vicki did not sing 'God Save the Queen'. Few people did.

Catafalque Party move off. Troops move off. Ceremony closes.

ADVANCE AUSTRALIA FAIR.

The crowd obeyed. They sang 'Advance Australia Fair' which is described, I believe, as our national song. But it is a song filled with so many lies and errors of fact and it is not our real song and never was. Our real song is the song about the swagman who stole a sheep and committed suicide rather than be arrested. It does not misdescribe our sterile soil or claim we are young and free but it is the song of our heart. It was not written in Sydney but its spirit was born where we were presently assembled with the Tank Stream flowing like a dirty secret underneath our feet. It is 'Waltzing Matilda' that we cannot paint out, the template that shapes even those who feel beyond it. The past is never dead, wrote William Faulkner, it is not even past. In 'Waltzing Matilda' we are at our best. We do not have a Statue of Liberty but when we sing, when we thereby imaginatively inhabit the world of 'Waltzing Matilda', we become all the poor and all the down-trodden. It is not a song of triumph but of empathy. It suits us. We can be very confident that the men who died at Gallipoli loved that song, and it is not just the RSL who is too embarrassed, too prim, too bureaucratic to remember it.

After the service the five of us walked very slowly through the streets named after British naval officers and prime ministers, past the two big state government buildings, the larger one named for Phillip, the smaller one for Macquarie, and we drove down by the wharves at Woolloomooloo, past the entrance to the Garden Island

Naval Dockyard, up the hill to Macleay Street to the one part of Sydney we expected to be still awake. But Kings Cross at six in the morning was not a pretty sight, and whatever excitement or tawdry glamour it commonly borrows from drugs and criminals and prostitution was not available at this hour. Still, the Bourbon and Beefsteak was open and young men and women in dirty denim were staggering from its wide door into the street.

Come on, said Fix, let's get some steak and eggs.

No, said Kelvin, the food is shithouse.

But we drifted uncertainly into the entrance where a dangerous-looking bouncer was shepherding a crying woman out into the street. Downstairs a band was playing, but we stepped sideways into the restaurant which was decorated with incongruous British-looking bric-à-brac, incongruous because the owner of the Bourbon and Beefsteak was a former US naval intelligence officer, a partner of the Nugan Hand Bank, a CIA front which is commonly reputed to have played an active role in destabilising our elected government in 1975.

Let's go, said Kelvin. Let's go up the road to Bar Coluzzi.

Mate, this is a perfect complement to Anzac Day.

How's that? asked Vicki.

In 1915 we gave our blood for the British; exactly sixty years later we sacrificed our government to the Americans. This is one of the places where the deed was done.

The service is bad and the food is lousy. Not even the Mafia would eat in a place like this, said Kelvin, looking around at the marooned diners who had been abandoned with no comfort other than that provided by a laminated menu and a glass of tepid water.

We drank our water. We read our menus. Half an hour later, still not having placed an order, we left the Bourbon and Beefsteak and walked through the wet streets on a bickering search for breakfast.

Bar Coluzzi, a place where we would normally expect to see many of our friends, was shut. So we settled for Tropicana just across the road and there the five of us ate bacon and eggs, and talked and drank coffee and watched the television and drank more coffee. But no matter how much coffee we drank I cannot manufacture enough cups to justify my memory that it was on the flickering television in Tropicana that we saw John Howard appear. It was just before dawn on Gallipoli and there he was, together with the Turkish prime minister and thousands of young

Australians who had travelled to make remembrance on Turkish soil.

It was in Tropicana, without a doubt, that we saw our prime minister speak. We heard him say we were comrades with the Turks today. This long-ago event would live with us for ever. It had been the making of our nation, and for once, just briefly, I did not feel myself his enemy.

Then I looked at Vicki and saw the tears welling in her eyes, and it was only then I understood the bitter irony of this moment.

Our prime minister could embrace and forgive the people who killed our beloved sons and fathers, and so he should, but he could not, would not, apologise to the Aboriginal people for 200 years of murder and abuse. The battle against the Turks, he said in Gallipoli, was our history, our tradition. The war against the Aboriginals, he had already said at home, had happened long ago. The battle had made us; the war that won the continent was best forgotten.

Hearing the prime minister speak, Vicki bowed her head and began searching in her handbag. I thought she was looking for a tissue, but instead she produced a slim pair of nail scissors. By the time she had removed the medals from her jacket, her eyes had become curiously cold. Very carefully, one might say thoughtfully, she removed the ribbons from each decoration and cut them into strips as thin as string.

We old white men said nothing. What could we say? We watched as she swept the ribbons into her open hand and dropped them into a polystyrene cup.

Sheridan looked down at his own two medals.

Don't, said Fix.

Sherry's big hands fluttered over the medals as if he planned to do the same.

Don't, said Vicki. Please, just don't.

CHAPTER TWENTY-FIVE

HOW CAN I HOPE to convey to any reader my idea of Sydney? I have seen nothing to equal it in the way of landlocked scenery, in the particular relationship between the races, in the easy tolerance of crime and corruption, in the familiar mingling you can witness on the footpath outside Bar Coluzzi any morning, where you may find judges and writers and the euphemistically labelled 'colourful racing identities' all bunched happily together in the sunshine, somehow feeling themselves to be at the red-hot centre of the town. On the wall inside you can see photographs of George Foreman, Clive James and Claudia Cardinale.

Jack Ledoux would not have described himself as part of any crowd, let alone this one, but he was a regular at Bar Coluzzi and it was here we met to say goodbye on the day of my departure.

I had by now given up all hope of getting his story, but I was happy to be meeting here because it seemed so very expressive of the town's character, because it seemed connected, by long, long threads of custom, to the first day of the colony.

I carried to this meeting a newspaper article from the *Daily Telegraph* on December 23 1999, and this seemed a very rich document to me and one which I had highlighted in the places which are italicised below.

Former coffee-shop owner Luigi Coluzzi yesterday escaped a full-time jail sentence for bashing a man unconscious on Darlinghurst's café strip last year.

NSW district court judge Brian Wall instead ordered Coluzzi, 34, to serve two years periodic detention for assaulting artist Max Droga outside Bar Coluzzi on Victoria Street on January 23.

Judge Wall said yesterday that it was a violent attack at the upper end of the scale of grievous bodily harm.

He found Coluzzi had deliberately, rather than recklessly, caused serious injury to Mr Droga, and on the objective facts he deserved to be jailed.

But under the subjective circumstances – that Droga had harassed him for five years and that Coluzzi had *a 'very vulnerable personality'* – he opted for the lighter sentence.

The bad blood between Coluzzi and Droga, the *Telegraph* later reported, dates back to 1989 when *Coluzzi smashed an aggressive dog over the head with a baseball bat, killing it*, outside Bar Coluzzi.

Four years after the event, local *coffee-lover* Max Droga began taunting Coluzzi, calling him a '*dog-killer*' and 'psychopath' every time they crossed paths.

On January 23 last year, after more jibes *and five years of restraint*, Coluzzi snapped and began swinging punches at Droga as stunned customers looked on.

At least one of his punches connected, knocking Droga unconscious and head first into the pavement, causing him serious head injuries. *Droga was rushed to St Vincent's and later underwent a partial lobotomy.*

During the three-week trial, café owners from Victoria Street, some of their customers, an Olympic boxer and even ABC [Australian Broadcasting Corporation] boss David Hill gave evidence.

I despair of being able to explain all this, I

told Jack Ledoux, but it seems somehow that this is where the book should end, here on this footpath, with everyone eating their focaccia and drinking their lattes and espresso. I should read you this article and then we should discuss it.

Jack did not say a thing for a while but looked away from me, and I knew I had offended him with my negativity.

You know, Peter, he said at last, this is not owned by the Coluzzi family any more.

Yes, but the clientèle is just the same. There is this same mixture of legal power and art and people who are, shall we say, less than legal.

Yes, but you see, Peter, you're missing so much that is wonderful about this town. You told me the story of Vicki and her father's medals.

Surely you're not saying that these stories should not be told?

No, no, of course not, but it's a question of balance. You're the chap, remember, who arrived here a month ago and all you wanted to do was collect stories of Earth and Air and Fire and Water.

Well, Jack, some people made that difficult . . .

You lost your batteries, he reminded me. Do you have them now?

I do, yes.

If I tell you this story will you at least put it after the Coluzzi story, and after the medals?

You want a happy ending.

Well, I don't know how happy it is, he laughed. I very nearly died.

CHAPTER TWENTY-SIX

YOU WANT THE STORY of the southerly, said Jack Ledoux, but first I have to tell you about the Hawkesbury River.

The headwater of the Hawkesbury is near Goulburn, right over to the south-west of Sydney, and the river travels around the city almost in a circle. At Wisemans Ferry it heads east towards the coast. When it finally spills out into the sea it is about twenty miles north of the harbour bridge.

And when I say it spills out into the sea, there are times when it actually *boils* out into the sea.

This estuary is very aptly named Broken Bay because there's an immense chunk *broken* out of the coast, leaving a mouth about eight miles wide. There's Cape Three Points to the north and Barrenjoey to the south.

Then, inside the mouth, there's this worn and weathered sandstone remnant – Lion Island. This lion is couchant, its gruff head pointing out to sea. It's a bird sanctuary and you're not allowed on shore, but if you sneak up the lee side by the beach you can climb the back of the lion and sleep in the caves at the top.

Sometimes it's like a bloody millpond around Lion Island – polished surface, first hint of a nor'-easter coming in the morning, God's own place. But at other times when there has been heavy rain – and Sydney is subtropical so twelve inches of rain in three days is nothing to us – then all that weight of water gathers in the Hawkesbury and this brown liquid *spews* itself out into the ocean *and* if this happens at a time when there is a strong easterly on-shore gale blowing against that tidal stream *and* if it happens that the tide is also running out, then it is a place of ultimate evil. If you're in a small boat you should know enough to stay away.

But this story is not just about a southerly buster, it's about a very particular boat, so let me tell you why that boat came into being.

Anybody who doesn't have a boat in Sydney is not a citizen of Sydney. Well, that's my opinion, but if you're on Pittwater it's beyond opinion. You have no cars, no roads – you leave them behind at Church Point and travel home across the water by ferry, water taxi, or tinny. You know what a tinny is? A beat-up aluminium dinghy with a thirty-hp engine on the back. I've had plenty of tinnies but in 1984 I finally designed a wooden boat.

Now I've lived on Pittwater for nearly forty years but I've been sailing for even longer, since I was nine years of age. Most of that time was spent in racing boats, and in racing boats you don't carry *anything* along for the ride. Everything has to be pared back to the absolute bloody minimum. So I set out to design a boat that was the culmination of all that experience, but a boat that would also be wonderful for Pittwater.

Which means it had to be not only a sailing boat but it also had to row. And that's a hard equation because a sailing boat needs stability, and a rowing boat has to be long and thin and fine so it can be pulled through the water. It needs *instability*.

The plans I finally delivered to the boat builder bridged these two qualities.

They were for a skiff, nineteen foot three overall, eighteen foot six on the waterline. She would be five foot gunwale to gunwale. She would draw eight inches with a hollow garboard. And her sections would be like a wine glass.

I designed a very fine bow, but I also gave her a fine stern. So the boat would be able to go in both directions. She would go through the water with the minimum of resistance and she would have a very fine sailing rig in her. She'd have a fully battened mainsail so when you saw her against the light, the ribs would show like a dragonfly wing. She'd have no centreboard or keel but leeboards to stop her being pushed sidewards by the wind. That would permit you to sneak up into the shallow creeks and estuaries, and because there would be no centreboard two of you would be able to sleep in the bottom of the boat, watch the birds early in the morning, and so forth.

It took seven weeks for my mate Stumpy to build her and it took me a year and a half to finish her off. She was made of three eighth-of-an-inch-thick skins of Australian red cedar, cross-laminated, epoxy glued and unbelievably strong. I named her *Dorothy*, after my mother.

Dorothy was light, built like an eggshell, and she sailed wonderfully, but the way you kept her up was with your bodyweight. So she was dangerous, not by accident, but by design.

At the time of this story, friends of mine had built this *beautiful* small house up the reaches of the

Hawkesbury about fifteen miles up from Lion Island. And I sailed up there one January afternoon. Beautiful weather. Nor'-easterly wind. I went up like a bloody flash. I passed the little waterfront village of Bar Point and everybody saw me going hurtling past and gave a great wave. *That's a nice-looking little boat.* They knew what they were looking at.

About nightfall I finally got up this tiny little creek where my friends live and I thought, I won't go ashore now, I'll sleep in the boat.

I had a great night's sleep and went on to have a wonderful day with my friends. But from the moment I opened my eyes next morning I saw we were in for a southerly change. In Sydney you always get twenty-four hours' notice of a southerly. You'll have what *looks* like a very clear day, but high up you might notice those mare's tails of cirrus clouds. These are the top part of a wedge of cold air being driven up by the front. These clouds will stretch for about six hundred miles, which equates to about twenty-four hours. What I'm saying is, the southerly was not a surprise to me. When I saw those mare's tails I knew it was coming. And I also knew, even then, lying in my boat, there was the real possibility of it being severe. It had been so hot and muggy.

These storms always begin from the south-west. Then they slowly shift around to the south, then to the south-east and then over the next few days they break to the east and the north-east. And when, finally, the wind shifts to the north-west you know the cycle is setting itself up again. That's the summer pattern in Sydney.

So the first stage of the cycle began on my second night upriver. A south-westerly.

When I woke next morning there was a strong southerly blowing. I looked up and saw these grey clouds moving like a conveyor belt and they were *fast*. Looked like thirty knots to me.

Oh, fuck, well I'll probably be OK.

I had expected it would be fast, but as I got out on to the river proper, I saw it was really *piping*. Thirty knots in the tropics is nothing, but thirty knots in a southerly is something different. Southerly air is polar maritime. It's thicker, colder, wetter. It's got more grunt.

So I *flew* down that bloody river. I had a *hair-raising* ride. I went *planing* through the water-front village of Brooklyn and through Bar Point again. The same people who had waved to me going up now saw this joker *flying* fucking past them. I barely had hands to wave.

I went under the Brooklyn Bridge at a rate of fucking knots. I went *haring* around the point at bloody Brooklyn and this is an open boat so it

takes a bit of water and when you're going that
fast there's a lot of spray around.

All the time the wind is across the river. That's
OK, I'm not going into the wind. And the wind is
not going against the tide. But this boat is a
handful to sail at the best of times, so what
you've got to do to *pump* it, you have to hold
the mainsheet (which is the rope that holds the
mainsail) in your teeth. You've got your feet
under the straps. You're out over the side. You're
steering with this hand and you've got your
pumps hooked up so you can work them with
your left hand. So you're like one of these jokers
on the street corner with five musical instru-
ments. With your right foot you're beating
drums. With your left foot you're cracking wal-
nuts. And you're flying down the river.

As I come down towards the opening, the river
is getting much wider. There's been a lot of rain
in the storm so there's a lot of brown water
travelling towards the sea. There's also a high
tide that's moving out, and the wind is moving to
the south, and I know that the fucking southerly
swell must be starting to come round Barrenjoey.

And I think, *oh shit*.

At the same time I think, *so far so good*.

And I go around Juno Point which is maybe
two or three miles before the entry to the estuary.

The tide rips around it and I am flying. The tide is doing four knots, easy, so that's an *extra* four knots added to my speed. *What a sail this is.*

By this time I have been going for two hours and I am getting tired and I see, in the lee of the shore on the south side of the river, that boats are sheltering. And I see a mate of mine, a mooring-lifter, and I know I've still got this dangerous estuary to negotiate and I think, *I better pull out now. I'll get a tow back with him.*

But I am getting closer and closer to home territory. *So far so good.*

I am heading towards West Head by this time and I can see Lion Island ahead of me. There's a big sea. The waves are breaking on the 'bow' of the island, and they are exploding on the rocks and cascading up the cliffs.

So I think, *it's OK, I can sneak in close to the shore . . .*

The water is disturbed by the wind blowing against the tide. It's turned a really nasty colour, a filthy grey-green. The sky is leaden. And as I come past Flint and Steel Beach in the driving rain I begin to have second thoughts. *I might just whip in there and wait it out.*

But no, I could fucking beat the world by this time. And I had a date with Brigit that night in the city.

Until this time I have been 'reaching', with the wind across the boat. But as I come into the opening of Pittwater, the wind is coming out like the mouth of a fucking trumpet. It is blowing forty knots and it is increasing.

I think, *fuck*, but it is too late. I can't turn around now even if I want to. I'm to the south of Lion Island and the wind is blowing from the south, so if I stop I'll be blown on to the rocks.

So, my only choice is get across the mouth of Pittwater, and I can tack under Barrenjoey head-land and then I plan to sneak around the Joey and perhaps, with luck, on to the beach there. There are rain squalls and there isn't a bugger around anywhere. My big ambition now is to just make it to that beach in one piece.

I am pumping the bloody boat all the time and I get all the way across the mouth of Pittwater. I get under Barrenjoey. I tack. I start to work out under the Joey when I see this gust coming. It is blowing so hard it takes the spray right off the top of the water. As it comes it *turns* and it *twists*.

Holy shit.

It picks me up and just dumps me straight in the drink.

My boat filled straight away. I was awash. Completely fucked. My sleeping bag started to drift

off, my kit bag, my sketchbooks. The boat tipped
upside down. The rudder fell out.

Well I can't swim, and besides, the golden rule
of sailing boats is *stay with the boat*. So I hung
on.

Slowly, of course, the wind pushed me out of
the shelter of Barrenjoey and then I began to be
carried out by the tide. And these great southerly
seas were running around Barrenjoey. Ten-,
maybe twelve-foot waves. And naturally the
bottom of the boat had been rubbed back to a
racing finish. And as my mate Beetle said to me
afterwards, *I could see the fingernail marks on
the bottom of the boat*. Finally I was hanging on
to one of the leeboards, but I got further and
further out and the seas got bigger and bigger. By
now it was about three in the afternoon. I was
getting colder and tireder and I began getting
washed off the boat. The waves were like surf
waves. And I'd be washed off and I'd get back on
board again and I'd be washed off. And the only
thing I can remember, as I realised how serious
this was, is *anger*, absolute fucking *anger*. It was
almost the only thing that kept me warm.

I could occasionally see Pittwater appearing
through the weather and I knew my mother's
little place was down there and she, my boat's

namesake, was quietly watching the television with a Scotch beside her.

But I'd blown it. I'd fucking blown it through absolute stupidity. And the tide was dragging me further and further out and I was starting to head for the mincer. I mean, Lion Island, where me and my boat would be smashed to pieces on the rocks.

And I thought, *that's it*.

And: *you're a fuckwit*.

So I just hung on, hoping for a miracle. Then I began to think I could see something. There was a great rain squall coming out of Pittwater and through it I could see *something*. Whatever it was, it was disappearing, then appearing, then disappearing. I thought it couldn't be a boat, but it was, a motor-boat, not heading up the river, but out to sea. I thought, what sort of an *idiot* would come out in this sort of weather?

But it came closer, and closer, and closer. And finally I could see it clearly – a 35-footer – and you know I never liked those hot-water boats, but here it was, *Jennifer*, with this tiny little fellow up there on the flying bridge. And he was towing a dinghy which *proved* he was in-sane. You never *ever* tow a dinghy in high seas, because the dinghy will swamp and then you are in real strife.

So here am I, about to drown, and I'm thinking, *oh Jesus, this bloke's mad.*

But also *he's going to save me.*

Jennifer was now almost on top of me. She was raising up on these huge waves and crashing back down again but she came alongside me and as she came down on a wave I *grabbed* hold of the bow and it *swung* back up into the air and *Jennifer* lifted me up off *Dorothy* like a bloody crane.

I had hypothermia. I was exhausted but I lifted myself up bodily on to the bow of his boat. And I staggered down towards my rescuer.

Why? I asked him. *Why did you come out here?*

I was up in the bloody estuary, he says, and this storm come through and I thought somebody might be in trouble so I come out to take a look.

My saviour's name was Stratmore Garside. He was a real character, the smallest of all God's angels. He gave me his clothes to put on. His pants came up to here on me. And a little tiny sweater. He saved my life. Then he got the water police on the radio so they could save my boat.

Of course the water police are local people. And they came out like a flash. They were just brilliant. But when they saw little Stratmore with his hot-water boat and his dinghy they must have recognised a disaster waiting to unfold.

For Christsake get the fucking hell out of here.

Stratmore was offended by this message on the radio. *What's the matter, can't they see how I'm handling it?*

What a wonderful character. As soon as I got home, or the next morning – because that's when you draw best – I did a drawing for him of the scene. Really rough charcoal, but the sense of a storm and the boat coming out of the mist. He was just terrific, this guy, although the cops were right – he should have just turned around and come in, but he was fearless and he stayed with *Dorothy* until the police arrived.

For Christsake get the fucking hell out of here.

He was offended but he obeyed, although not before I had witnessed my great mate Bowsey jump off the police launch into those screaming seas. He got a rope around my boat and then they towed her. Side on! At twelve knots! By God, you should see the photograph – the entire boat is out of the water.

My boat survived the rescue and my life was saved, so you'd think I'd be content, but I soon began to dwell upon that missing rudder. Such a lot of time and care had gone into its manufacture. And I began to think, if the tide was running out and the southerly wind was blowing in, and if the tide was about to change, then my rudder *might* have been taken out to sea and it *might* have been carried north and gotten washed up on the beaches north near Ettalong.

Of course, it might just as easily have been smashed on the rocks on Lion Island, but I phoned my mate Fisho who lives at Woy Woy. I asked him if he would put an advertisement in the local rag.

In less than a week he was back on the phone. *A bloke's rung me, he's got your rudder.*

You got to be joking.

Fisho explained how this bloke was fishing at low tide, way up the coast, near Gosford, and he slipped on something under the weeds.

As it happened, he was also a member of a local crafts movement. He was a *woodworker* and when he saw the red mahogany, he knew its worth. What he now had in his hands was a laminated centre rudder blade – spotted gum in the centre part of the rudder head, cedar cheeks, laminated Australian beech tiller curve. *My lucky day*, he thought. He took it home and put it on his mantelpiece.

Then the poor bugger read Fisho's ad in the local newspaper. That was a cruel test of

character, which he passed with flying colours.
Just the same he was not exactly *delighted* to hear
from me.

Describe the rudder to me.

And I did.

Just my luck.

I can't tell you how grateful I am.

I bet you can't.

Do you mind if I come and pick it up?

No.

What can I bring you?

A bottle of Inner Circle rum.

So I found a bottle of Inner Circle rum, and
went to a warehouse in Gosford where this bloke
worked as a storeman and packer.

And he handed over the rudder.

And I paid in the oldest currency of all.

And that's the end of the story.

A NOTE ON THE TYPE

The text of this book is set in Linotype Sabon, named after the type founder, Jacques Sabon. It was designed by Jan Tschichold and jointly developed by Linotype, Monotype and Stempel, in response to a need for a typeface to be available in identical form for mechanical hot metal composition and hand composition using foundry type. Tschichold based his design for Sabon roman on a fount engraved by Garamond, and Sabon italic on a fount by Granjon. It was first used in 1966 and has proved an enduring modern classic.